Also by Florence Isaacs
Just a Note to Say . . .
Business Notes
Toxic Friends/True Friends

My Deepest Sympathies...

My Deepest Sympathies...

*Meaningful Sentiments for
Condolence Notes and Conversations,
Plus a Guide to Eulogies*

Florence Isaacs

Clarkson Potter/Publishers
New York

Published by Clarkson Potter/Publishers, New York, New York.
Member of the Crown Publishing Group.

Random House, Inc. New York, Toronto, London, Sydney, Auckland
www.randomhouse.com

CLARKSON N. POTTER is a trademark and Potter and colophon
are registered trademarks of Random House, Inc.

Printed in the United States of America

Design by Jan Derevjanik

Library of Congress Cataloging-in-Publication Data
Isaacs, Florence.
    My deepest sympathies : meaningful sentiments for condolence
notes and conversations, plus a guide to eulogies / by Florence
Isaacs.—1st ed.
    Includes bibliographical references.
    1. Condolence notes—Handbooks, manuals, etc.   I. Title.
BJ2115.C65 I83 2000
395.4—dc21   99-059905

ISBN 0-609-60565-8

10 9 8 7 6 5 4 3 2 1

First Edition

To Harvey,
always there

Acknowledgments

Many people contributed to this book, providing a wealth of information I couldn't have done without. I especially wish to thank Suzy Powell, a great lady; my friend Sam Perelson of Perelson Weiner CPAs; and Frank Gribbon, editor, *Fire Lines,* Uniformed Firefighters Association of Greater New York. Your input added immeasurably to this project. I thank my colleague Pat McNees, author of *Dying: A Book of Comfort,* for generously sharing her experiences. As always, family therapist Karen Gail Lewis, Ed.D., coeditor of *Siblings in Therapy* was extraordinarily helpful. I thank Mary Jo Dahm for her aid.

For their insights, I also thank Chris Ulrich, C.S.W., Long Island Jewish Medical Center; Camille Wortman, Ph.D., professor of psychology, State University of New York at Stony Brook; Susan Kavaler-Adler, Ph.D., clinical psychologist in private practice in Manhattan and author of *The Compulsion to Create* and *Mourning and Psychic Transformation: Facing the Demon Lover Within;* Kenneth Doka, Ph.D., coauthor of *Grief Beyond Gender;* Bruce Patterson, C.S.W.; grief counselor Nancy Burns; Reverend Robert Corin Morris, director, Interweave; Henry M. Seiden, Ph.D., coauthor of *Silent Grief: Living in the Wake of Suicide;*

Stephanie LaFarge, Ph.D., director of counseling services, ASPCA of New York; Ann Douglas, coauthor of *The Unofficial Guide to Having a Baby;* Jean Coffey; Iman Yusuf Hasan, staff chaplain, Memorial Sloan Kettering; Sister Janet Baxendal; and Rabbi Harlan J. Wechsler, Congregation Or Zarua.

I also thank, for their invaluable assistance, George Burke, International Association of Firefighters; John Horan, president, Horan & McConaty Funeral Service/Cremation, Aurora, CO; John Carmon, Carmon Community Funeral Homes, Windsor CT; The Health Care Chaplaincy; and The Compassionate Friends.

Contents

Introduction

The blank sheet of notepaper sits on your desk for days, as you obsess over what to write to a former coworker whose wife died in an auto accident. No wonder you can't pick up a pen. What can you write when a mother of three dies at forty-five? If you call— or go to the funeral—what can you possibly say to the grieving husband? It's no easier when your friend's ninety-year-old father succumbs to heart failure. What is there to say when the person has lived to old age and the death is not unexpected (or unwelcome in some cases)? Yet someone you care about has lost her father—and everything that comes to mind sounds like a cliché.

If the dilemma sounds familiar, you're not alone. Strong men squirm at the task of extending sympathy to someone who has lost a loved one. Women, who are normally more expressive, feel uncertain and often tongue-tied. Why does someone else's grief make us so uneasy? We feel helpless in the face of profound loss. Death is as final as you get. There's nothing that can be done to change it—and we don't know what to do about that.

Someone else's loss forces us to confront the subject of death. Although many other cultures view death as a natural part of the life cycle, death is not a welcome subject in a society geared to the young, the healthy, and the beautiful. Many of us have grown up without experiencing the death of someone close. People live longer; medical advances have tamed many killer diseases. We do not commonly see spouses, siblings, children, or others die around us as our grandparents and even our parents' generation did.

When death does take someone we love, we are removed from it. People used to die at home, cared for until the very end by their families. As an accepted part of life, death was far less mysterious. People not only lived with the entire process, they were also surrounded and nourished by the support of relatives and community. Often, it was the family that prepared the body for burial. There was a close connection with the death—a full experience that provided strength and comfort to survivors. As people began to die in hospitals rather than at home, however, and funeral homes handled the rest, we became distanced from the process. Death became more frightening, something to be whispered about, tiptoed around, rather than openly acknowledged.

A death in someone else's family also stirs our own deepest fears of mortality—and of losing those *we* love. It's a reminder that *our* parent or spouse or child can be taken. If our own families were a poor role model in dealing with death, that adds to feelings of insecurity. When I was growing up, a death was talked about in hushed tones as if there was something to hide, as if the person grieving might shatter into pieces if the deceased was mentioned. Yet to pretend that death hasn't really happened is to isolate us rather than bring us together.

In my family, feelings about the loss were never discussed. Funerals were considered "for adults only," which added to a generalized fear. Years ago when my best friend's father died, I felt so anxious about attending the funeral I managed to show up late. The hearse was pulling away from the curb as I arrived, and deep down, I felt relieved. It was a tribute to my friend's devotion that she was able to understand and forgive me.

Of course we also fear that we will make a mistake, say or do something wrong, and make matters worse for the bereaved. Today, it's easier than ever to err no matter how well-intentioned we try to be. Myths about what is or isn't helpful to the grieving family can lead you astray. Situations that didn't exist years ago add to the confusion:

- *Social changes have created delicate situations.* Couples are no longer necessarily married. The bereaved may be a significant other or a companion. The person who died may be a stepparent or stepchild, or an ex-wife or ex-husband.

- *Our society is multicultural.* You may be expressing sympathy to someone from a culture and/or religion that you know little or nothing about. A colleague who grew up in Pakistan may have lost a brother. A neighbor originally from Japan may have lost her child. A friend who was raised in a Jewish household, but is no longer observant, loses a parent. The husband of someone from Vietnam may have died. The normal discomfort that surrounds news of a death is compounded when you don't know the customs of the bereaved.

- *More people live with chronic disease for long periods.* The deceased may have suffered for years with cancer or Alzheimer's. The death may look like a blessing for all concerned—both the deceased and those who survive.

These and other situations can feel like a minefield. You don't want to insult or alienate people, or embarrass yourself. Fortunately, there are ways to cut through the anxiety and do what's right. You can find words for condolence notes and other expressions of sympathy. You can feel confident that you are behaving appropriately every time. The pages that follow will show you how.

There isn't any magic involved. It's simply a matter of knowing what's going on. When you understand what the bereaved is likely to be experiencing (and likely to need)—and your own reactions to what has happened—you can stop feeling awkward and inadequate.

The loss of a loved one stirs all kinds of emotions in those left behind. Issues vary, depending on who has died (losing a sister is different from losing a father), how the person died, the quality of the relationship between bereaved and deceased, and many other factors. Each chapter ahead explores relevant psychological and practical issues, arming you with the information and skills you need.

You'll find advice on everything from correct phrasing in condolence notes and conversations to suitable context, plus examples to stimulate your own thinking. Included are rules for expressing regret at different kinds of relationship losses, what you need to know about funerals, memorial services, and other events, plus answers to questions such as "Should I send flowers?" "How much should I contribute?" "Should I go to the burial?"

You'll learn simple techniques for eulogies, which have grown increasingly common in recent years. Many believe (erroneously) that you need a special talent to write and deliver a tribute. In fact, all you need is a heart. What touches people is sincerity. Practical tips will show you how to shape warm salutes that work for personal, business, or professional situations.

Occasions when you need to respond to a death arise all the time on the job, in the family, in the community—and there has never been a more important time to know your way around them. Technology and our high-speed lives have increased isolation, eroded personal contact, and flattened rituals that support and bring us together. A death in someone's family becomes an opportunity to connect. It presents obligations to do what is right. It also allows us to affirm our bonds as human beings.

In our "can do," youth-oriented society, we feel less and less comfortable with issues of growing older and dying. Confronted with a death, we don't know what to do. But when you understand what is expected of you (it's a lot less than you think) and how to respond, you can relax and do the right thing even in the toughest, tensest situations. With the easy guidelines that follow, you'll never feel intimidated again.

Lessons in
Condolence Notes

At a recent checkup, I told my dentist that I was writing a book on condolences. Intrigued, he mentioned that his mother had died two years earlier. "I got some wonderful notes from friends *and* from patients," he told me. "I've still got them. Let me show you." He reappeared minutes later with a fistful of cards and letters.

His response is not unusual. Condolence messages mean a great deal to people, so much so that the bereaved tend to keep them. Months or even years later, the person may pull them out, reread them, and remember who took the time and made the effort to write.

Most of us, however, dread writing words of sympathy. Yet it is important to extend condolences if you care about the person who has died and those who are left behind. Sometimes you are obligated to write for business or social reasons. Regardless of the situation, you *can* compose something personal and appropriate every time. The secret is sincerity and the ability to be yourself. When you loosen up and dare to trust your instincts, you free the flow of words that really matter.

The Goal of a Condolence Note

Some of the anxiety involved in writing condolences stems from misconceptions about the function of a note. You think that you have to *do* something to change what has happened or erase the pain of the survivor. Since that is impossible, you feel helpless. But there *is* something very important that you *can* do: you can communicate with the mourner and say, "I know what has happened. I care."

A good condolence note:

- Acknowledges the person's loss.
- Expresses your sympathy.
- In certain cases, it comforts.

Unless you know the bereaved (or knew the deceased) very well, however, you usually cannot console. Accept that. In general, attempts to comfort tend to be misguided and may be resented by the mourner.

The challenge is to personalize your words and say something meaningful. A good note reflects the recipient and the deceased. It conveys the message: "I know who you are and I know who you lost."

Personal Relationships

When my own father died, an acquaintance I'd known for many years added these lines to a printed card: "I'm sorry to hear of the loss of your loved one.

I extend my condolences." Although I appreciated the thought, the words could have been written by anyone —to anyone. Remember that it's your expression of caring that counts. At the very least you want to start off with "Dear Mary"—and mention the name of the deceased (if you know it). If not, you can say, "I'm sorry to hear of your husband's death." It makes a big difference.

The degree of intimacy between you and the bereaved helps dictate what you will write. Are you addressing a dear friend or family member, a distant relative, a neighbor? An obligatory note to someone you know at church will take a different approach from one directed to a beloved aunt.

Business Relationships

If the condolence is job-related, there's usually more distance. But the fact that you write says a lot. It tells the recipient, "You mean something as a person. You're more than merely a customer, employee, or coworker." Simple personalization underscores that you took the time and you care.

Be sure to get the facts straight, however, or a thoughtful gesture can wind up an embarrassment. After his mother died, one executive received a note from a supplier which expressed sorrow that she had died so soon after his father. In fact, the father's death had occurred fifteen years earlier. The person had either misread the obituary or didn't listen when he was told what had happened. In another case, someone extended condolences on the death of a sister when it was a brother who had died. These are the kinds of mishaps that can undo your good intentions.

What Should You Say?

The question can seem unanswerable, but the key is honesty, simplicity, and usually, brevity. Keep your note short unless you're very close to the people involved. In truth, there is very little you can say in most cases. The core of it is that you're thinking of them, feeling for them, and want them to know that they are not alone. Even two or three lines can be extremely powerful, as in, "I was sad to hear about Sue's death. I want you to know that I am thinking of you. I extend my sincerest condolences." These few words, which can work for virtually any situation, speak volumes. They say what people want to hear. It's when you "overdo" that you're most likely to drift into clichés and meaningless generalities, and are at risk of saying something insensitive.

Most of us cringe at the thought of mentioning "death" or "died" in a note. The words remind us of what we don't want to be reminded of, and we fear they will upset the bereaved. When I tallied almost one hundred condolence cards and notes received by a friend of mine after his father died, I found that only a few used the word in any form. Most people turned to euphemisms like "passed away" or "the loss of your father." But there's no getting away from it; the person died. The mourner *is* upset. I consciously use the word "death" in my own notes because it's direct and appropriate. However, I do admit it took some practice to get used to it. If it's too uncomfortable for you, then say whatever feels right. What's most important is to write that note.

The idea is not to copy "models," but to get in

touch with what your heart wants to say. That's what helps you individualize your message. Use the techniques that follow to trigger your thoughts and emotions and to help you write something meaningful.

Talk About the Deceased

Many people hesitate to speak directly about the person who died. Yet mourners want (and need) to hear about their loved one. Their deepest fear is that the person will be forgotten. Anything positive you can say is a gift of healing to survivors.

Acknowledge the circumstances. Pretending that something *didn't* happen isolates people and makes them more alone with their experience. The more specifically you tailor what you say to what the bereaved are going through, the more they feel you're connected to them. While you should avoid graphic language of any kind, it is appropriate to let the bereaved know you have some sense of what is going on, as in "I can't imagine how difficult it is to lose someone you love in this way. My heart goes out to you."

A good condolence note is a tribute to the deceased. It memorializes the person, and is very specific. "Wendy warmed us with her wit and generosity. Her loan got us through our mortgage crisis" makes a concrete reference to the difference this person made in your life. To jog your memory, make a list of words that come to mind, such as gentle, vivacious, fiery, passionate, outspoken, effective, talented, affectionate, loyal, dignified, dynamic, courageous, funny, adventurous, open, intelligent, dependable, wise. Even flaws (mentioned with affection) can convey the essence of the person, as in, "Your father was a stubborn man, but such a charming one."

One woman wrote about a friend, "Theresa was the most accepting person I ever met. I could tell her my deepest fears and craziest thoughts and feel safe." An obligatory note to the widow of a business acquaintance might read, "Bob was a leader in our field. He gave his time and energy to open markets for all of us. The industry won't be the same without him."

You can also discuss what was going on in the deceased's life, as in, "He was so enthused about his new job last week. It seems impossible that things could change so tragically."

If you didn't know the deceased, check the obituary for information you can use in a note. Then you can write something like "I never knew your father was so active in the Chamber of Commerce (or served in the Pacific in World War II, or was born in London)."

You can also talk about how much the person will be missed, as in, "I hope you can find solace in knowing how much Pete meant to us at Acme Inc." Or, "Pete's death diminishes everyone at Burns & Hanson."

What do you write when the deceased was someone you disliked, such as the obnoxious brother of your childhood friend? Take the high road. You want to be there for the bereaved, yet refrain from saying anything dishonest about the deceased. You can always find *something* positive to say, even if you have to focus on his impeccable taste in wine or his talent for backgammon. One man is partial to lines like "It's hard to imagine next Thanksgiving (or the office) without him" that allow the bereaved to assume the person will be missed.

Factor in What Has Happened

Did the person die of a stroke at ninety-nine, or of cancer at age six? Was the cause of death a madman on a rampage, or a fatal fall? The circumstances will have a profound effect on what you say. In a sudden death, life has been snatched away without warning. The survivors' world has shattered.

When a shocking calamity strikes, what people need most is caring. A note like this one could be written to a woman who lost her brother and her husband on the same day.

> *Dear ——,*
>
> *I just heard the news that John and Larry died on Tuesday. I can't imagine what you must be going through. They were both such wonderful men.*
>
> *I'm so very sorry. Please let me help in any way I can. I will call to see what I can do.*
>
> *Sincerely,*

You can also pay attention to your gut reaction, and use that. Ask yourself, "How do I feel about what has happened?" Then write it down, as in "Words seem like a thimble in the ocean." A useful and powerful line is "I don't know what to say." It speaks to the enormity of the loss and validates it.

Tragedies touch such a human chord that they bring an outpouring of emotion from others. When her husband died in a well-publicized plane crash, one woman received many cards and letters from strangers, including some from a man who had written to the church where the funeral service was conducted. "He was very sincere. He's written a letter to me every year on the anniversary of the accident," she told me.

Suicide is a taboo subject that carries shame and stigma in our society. Those left behind always feel, at some level, guilty and often directly or indirectly blamed for what has happened. They may feel angry at themselves for not recognizing signs that the person intended to die, or for not saying or doing something that might have made a difference. They may feel rage at the deceased for choosing to die.

What can you write to the bereaved in such a situation? The fears and upsets stirred in us by any death are magnified by a tragedy. "I cannot imagine what you are going through" is always appropriate. Then write what you feel, such as "This is a nightmare," or "This is beyond comprehension," or "This is an unbelievable tragedy. It's impossible to find the words." That's a potent statement because the recipient surely feels that what has happened is beyond reason.

Reach Back for Memories

Sometimes small, telling incidents are the "gems." You can say, "I'll always remember when your mother . . ." and relate a kind or charming or funny thing she did, such as baking a cherry pie (your favorite) for your tenth birthday. Little details add poignancy to what you write. Did Aunt June always wear high heels to the supermarket? You can paint a scene with lines like "Who can forget the way she walked down the canned soup aisle, looking like a socialite." The mourner is likely to smile and think, "That was her."

It's always nice to capture something special or important about the loved one that might not be known to the bereaved. For example, family members usually don't know much about their loved one's work life. If you're a coworker, you're in a unique position to tell them something they don't already know, such as "At the office Christmas party every year, it was Karen who would talk one of the salesmen into playing Santa Claus. She had the power of persuasion."

If you just tell the person an anecdote like that at the funeral, it is likely to be forgotten. The mourners are usually so overwrought that information can't really be processed. But a note has lasting value and can be referred to again later.

You can also mention how the person affected your life, as in "It was your father who gave me the idea to open my own video rental store."

Repeat What You've Been Told

This is an effective device, especially when you didn't know the deceased. You might write something like "You talked so often about Dick's dignity during treatment and his refusal to give up."

When a friend's eighty-four-year-old mother died after years of failing health, I wrote to him: "It's hard to believe it was only last week that you talked about her latest trip to the hospital and her continuing 'duel' with her aide. She was obviously a feisty lady and I admired her gumption. Know that I am thinking of you—and of her."

Or recreate a happy moment the mourner told you about, as in, "I remember you talking about the party plans for your thirtieth wedding anniversary. We're deeply sorry for this enormous loss." Or, "I remember the stories of how you and Cal hitchhiked through Europe after college." Then the bereaved can remind themselves that as long as their loved ones remain in their thoughts, they will be "alive."

Comment on the Bereaved's Relationship with the Person Who Has Died

You can write to someone, "I know how close you two were," and try to capture something unique about the relationship, such as "I was always in awe of your devotion. How lucky she was to have a daughter who took her on trips throughout the world and truly enjoyed her company as a friend." Or, "How many couples can work together all day long and still enjoy being with each other after hours. You and John made a family business work, both at home and at the office."

What if the deceased was abusive or otherwise destructive to the bereaved? It's dangerous to say anything negative about the deceased because the mourner's attitude toward the person may change after the death. It's common to idealize the one who has died. Stick to "I just heard about Libby. I'm sorry. I want you to know that you are in my thoughts."

You can also mention the mourner's efforts on behalf of the deceased, as in "Despite everything, you saw to it she was taken care of in every way," or "I know how often you dropped everything to take him to doctors." But make such statements only if you're certain the person *was* a loving son or adoring wife. Not everyone is dutiful or attentive.

Avoid Common Mistakes

We're all afraid of saying the wrong thing, and sometimes we do. To prevent that, beware of assumptions about the bereaved's thoughts, feelings, or actions. Don't tell someone, "You must be grieving," or "You must feel lonely," or "You will feel." Such statements ascribe feelings. The bereaved may not feel that way at all and may resent it. People grieve differently. If the deceased was ill for a long time, required constant care, and suffered, the survivor may feel relieved. Others may feel rage at being abandoned.

Omit any interpretation of the event, such as "It was bound to happen," or "It was time for her to go. She's in God's hands now," or "It was God's will." Such words can anger the bereaved. Avoid other lines that irritate people, like "Time heals all wounds." (Time alone doesn't.) "She isn't in pain anymore" may *seem* comforting. In fact, it minimizes the loss.

Never say, "I know how you feel" unless you've experienced an identical loss under identical circumstances. People feel that their grief (and their loss) is singular. That's why "I cannot imagine what you are going through" or "I cannot imagine your sorrow" are meaningful lines.

On the other hand, if you *have* had the same loss, you are in a unique position to provide invaluable support. Then you can say, "I've been through something very similar. If you ever want to talk, I'd be honored to share some of the things I've learned."

Sharing your common experiences can be helpful, but it's also tricky. The main criterion is: Is it warming and helpful to the bereaved? Self-disclosure is easier when it's brief and pointed. There should be a quality of "Here is why I'm telling you this." The story must be related in a way that validates the other person's grief, rather than saying, "Oh, yeah. I had this happen to me. It was far worse and I got better." You *can* write something like "I remember when my spouse died. I didn't think I could go on, and supportive friends really helped me. I want to be supportive for you."

As a general rule, do not say anything religious unless you know the people well and are certain it's appropriate. Religious tracts can make those who aren't religious (or are of another religion) very uncomfortable. Although some bereaved persons become more devout, others may reexamine or reject beliefs and turn away. A religious message can reinforce feelings of alienation from (or anger toward) God at this time.

Belated Condolence Notes

Write promptly. I try to do so within a few days of hearing about the death. Certainly don't let it go more than a few weeks. However, if the news didn't reach you until much later (or personal circumstances intervened), by all means write a belated note. Try something like, "We only just learned that Harry died. We send sincere condolences." Or, "I just heard the sad news about Zoe and want you to know we are thinking of you." Or, "I learned only today that you lost your father. Who can forget how dedicated you were in caring for him for so long. Your many loving friends are here for you." Or, "We heard about your sister shortly after our return from London. Please accept our sympathy."

Or, "I was in Phoenix when I learned of your mother's death. Sheila joins me in offering our condolences."

Tone

Whatever you write, try to trust yourself. Resist feelings of reluctance and intimidation and the urge to censor thoughts and feelings. When you stop succumbing to thoughts like "This will sound silly (or stupid)," you open the door to connection and genuine expression. Avoid "shoulds" and intellectually preconceived ideas of acceptable words; they only add to anxiety and result in stilted prose. The point is not to impress people with poetry but to be sincere. You want to sound like yourself, the way you'd sound if you were talking to the bereaved. If you're stuck, speak into a tape recorder to cut through to the "real you." You'll find the words flow more naturally.

The right poem or quote can be a meaningful device when you pick something that reflects the person or speaks to what has happened. This quote from Erik H. Erikson might fit for a courageous father: "Healthy children will not fear life if their elders have integrity enough not to fear death." I might add: "On that basis, Ron left a great legacy to his daughters."

Or consider this quote from Samuel Butler: "To die completely, a person must not only forget but be forgotten, and he who is not forgotten is not dead." It might be followed by a line like "By that measure, Brenda will live forever."

Appearance of the Note

Condolence notes should be handwritten (in blue or black ink), unless your writing is truly illegible. A formal condolence letter written by you as a representative of your company or institution can also be typed. Correspondence cards are the perfect stationery for both business and social situations. They're also small; you can't write more than four or five lines (and only on one side). Use something larger and there's the temptation to fill up the space when you really have little to say. A half sheet, which can be folded over once, also fits for business situations. Women can use a small informal foldover note for nonbusiness condolences.

To whom should you address a condolence note? Send it to the mourner you know. If it was the deceased you knew, rather than the family, send it to the closest relative (adding "and family" if you wish). When the bereaved is married, address your card or note to him or her, although you may want to mention the person's spouse, as in, "Please send our love to Amy." If the spouse was close to the deceased, you can address the condolence to "Mr. & Mrs. John Jones." Sign off with, "Warmly," "Sincerely," "With warmth and affection," "Most sincerely," "Fondly," "Love," "Love you all." Or simply sign your name.

E-mail condolence notes are not appropriate unless you are writing to someone to whom you wouldn't otherwise send a condolence message. But E-mail can be very useful for follow-up communication with (and support for) the bereaved. When a colleague of mine was distraught over the death of her sister, I sent E-mails every few days, saying, "Just wondering how you're doing (or how you're holding up)" or, "Just checking in. Remember, I'm here."

Using Condolence Cards

There's nothing like a separate note to make a first-class impression. If you prefer, however, you can add a few handwritten lines to a condolence card.

Research done by Hallmark confirms that a card is much more meaningful when it includes a personal note, sometimes triggering thoughts that lead to a treasured letter. Hallmark reports that Americans send about 125 million sympathy cards each year.

Be careful to choose something appropriate. Cards with the simplest, briefest messages are usually best, unless you know the person's tastes and are lucky enough to find a card that you know will touch the recipient.

Select a religious message only if you are certain the recipient will welcome it. These lines, added to a card, would be appropriate if they were addressed to a devout mourner: "May God's love surround you always."

When writing to people of different religions or cultures, just speak from the heart. You write the same caring words to a Muslim or Buddhist, for example, as you would to anyone else, and if you wish, include a promise of support. Let your human sensitivity guide you.

Offering Help

If you genuinely want to help in a tangible way, by all means say so in your note. Don't do it, however, unless you really plan to follow through. Be specific, as in, "Please let me pick up Bobby at school (or handle your supermarket shopping). I'll call to arrange it with you." Or, "Let me take the next XYZ Co. meeting off your hands. I'll call to see how you want it handled." Do not make statements like "Let me know if there is anything I can do." The person will never call you.

People *can* help in many ways. You can offer to assist with the red tape and paperwork surrounding a death: contacting life insurance companies, dealing with taxes, notifying credit card companies. An employer can provide extra time off or help with the workload and health insurance forms. Counseling may be available through an employee assistance program. Your note can say, "I have asked ———, head of our human resources department, to call in a few days to see how she can assist you with Jim's pension and other details."

Talking to the Bereaved

Some of the same principles involved in writing condolence notes apply when you speak to grieving survivors during a chance meeting on the street, at the office, during a visit at home, or on the phone. At the first contact, you want to acknowledge the death and express your sympathy, as in "I'm very sad to hear about your wife." Saying "I'm sorry" bears witness to the death. (People feel angry and hurt when their loss is ignored.) A hand on the person's arm communicates that you may not know the words but are trying to help. You don't have to *do* anything. Just your attention and presence conveys your concern.

After you say "I'm sorry," the person may express grief or despair. Some of us are afraid to hear it. But grief is a healthy, normal reaction to the loss of a loved one. Don't be put off by tears either. Crying is therapeutic—and it usually doesn't go on for very long. You don't have to say anything while the person sobs. Just be there.

Be a Good Listener

Following the initial "I'm sad to hear about Polly," you may feel at a loss for words. If so, simply state, "I don't know what to say." That says a great deal. Then stop and let the other person talk. The bereaved often wants to tell the story over and over again. Talking about the details helps the person cope.

One size does not fit all, however. People have different coping styles. Some want to talk; some don't, and just want their privacy. Don't intrude. To polish your active listening skills, be aware that body language sends a message. The way you sit or stand, your tone of voice, whether or not you look the person in the eye, your whole demeanor, communicates your interest and support. Don't look as if you can't wait to bolt through the door. Nod your head or say "uh huh" occasionally. These actions tell people you hear and understand them and encourages them to continue.

Don't fill the silence; get comfortable with it. Just sitting quietly with the person is being there, too. It's calming for both of you if you can surrender to it. Unfortunately, some people find silence unnerving and rush to fill it. I believe that is one of the times when people are most likely to say or do something inappropriate. They speak out of anxiety.

Widows and widowers, single parents, and others alone especially need people with whom to reminisce about the loved one. An eighty-four-year-old widow told me how comforting it was to talk to old friends when her husband died. They knew him much of his life and were able to discuss her children as well. She'll never forget two friends who called every day for the first two weeks of grieving. Without fail, they still call her every week.

In a case where I had never met the deceased (and it was clear that a grieving friend felt like talking), I commented, "I didn't know your mother. Tell me about her." These words encouraged her to reminisce, producing an outpouring of wonderful stories about a cherished parent.

Anniversary of a Death

People do appreciate hearing from you on the birthday of the person who died, or on the anniversary of the death—sad times when the bereaved tend to get preoccupied with the loss. You may want to put the date on your calendar. You don't have to say, "This is the day he died." Just write, "I'm thinking of you today." *They* know it's the day. (If you wish to be thoughtful to someone who works for or with you, send flowers on the anniversary.) Anytime is a good time to send a photo of the deceased, along with a note reading, "Just came across this wonderful picture of Jamie. She looks so happy. Thought you'd like to have it."

Death of a Parent

The death of a parent is an expected life cycle event, yet it's the loss of the most basic relationship. It's also the end of a part of the bereaved's identity, as someone's son or daughter. It involves confronting not just the sadness of losing a parent, but losing a part of oneself. For many people, there's an extra element: the loss of that "cushion," the person who always adored them.

Leave space for the person to have all kinds of different feelings that come up at a time like this. Never say, "Don't feel that way." It's important for the bereaved to feel they have the right to all emotions—and that those emotions can be shared. When a woman who was adopted as a baby lost her mother, a few people commented, "Well at least it's easier for you." It was not less painful. This was the only mother she knew.

To help you write something that matters, here are tips geared specifically to situations where a parent has died.

Consider the Parent's Age

As more and more parents live to a ripe old age, it's all too easy to write something like "She lived a long life." Resist the temptation. Such statements actually minimize the loss. Grieving children may feel it wasn't long enough to suit them, and may resent your words. But you can reflect on the deceased's longevity in other ways. One note spoke of age in the context of strength, for example. Written to a cousin-in-law, it read:

> *Dear ——,*
>
> *Gary and I are deeply saddened by your dad's death. I'm so glad I got to know your parents when Gary and I first met. I always felt welcome around your entire family.*
>
> *May you reflect upon the strength that your dad possessed to make it to ninety-nine years. And may that strength shed light upon you to make it through this difficult time. We hope that the love and support of friends and family will bring you comfort.*
>
> *With love,*

Another approach that refers to long life might be: "Your mother was quite a woman. Her eighty-five years were well spent giving her love to others."

Is the Other Parent Still Living?

If the second parent has died, the adult child has completely lost a role as a son or daughter and has become the older generation. Because the person can feel truly alone, he or she is likely to appreciate a line like "Remember that your friends are here for you."

Of course there are also times when a parent's death comes much too early. The younger the person is when a mother or father dies, the greater the feeling of missing experiences. Bereaved who are young parents themselves mourn the milestones that the mother or father will never see in their own children. They mourn the future life they expected to have with the parent. This loss can be reflected in a note.

A woman pregnant with her first child when her forty-eight-year-old mother died received this note:

> *Dear ———,*
>
> *I have no words to tell you of my sorrow. Your mother was my dear friend and is simply irreplaceable.*
>
> *She would have been a wonderful grandmother. She was so gentle and had so much love to give. She was thrilled that you were expecting. You and her future grandchild meant everything to her.*
>
> *She will live in all our memories.*
>
> *With deep sympathy and love,*

Know What's Going On

Parent-child relationships can be very complicated. That's why it's important not to project your own feelings onto the bereaved. You may worship the ground *your* mother walks on, but others may feel differently.

Unless you know the mourner very well (and are certain it's true), avoid gushing about "your love" or "your enormous sorrow" or saying, "I know you must be grieving." Not everyone is upset—and it makes the person feel lonelier if nobody is even hinting at ambivalent feelings. It may embarrass the bereaved if others think they're not entitled to their feelings.

If you don't know the person well (or when in doubt), simply say, "I'm so sorry to hear of your father's death. I'm thinking of you."

Simplicity worked in lines that were added to a condolence card, written to someone who lost a father with whom she'd had a difficult relationship: "You are in my heart always. Love and hugs!" The writer, a childhood friend of the bereaved, knew all the details. The affection was welcome; leaving so much unspoken was powerful here.

How do you respond to a stepparent's death? If the person had a cool or hostile relationship with the stepparent, I wouldn't write at all. If they were close, I'd handle it as I would the death of a loved relative or friend, as in "I know that the two of you forged a close and affectionate relationship over the years. I extend deep sympathy."

If You Know the Relationship Was Positive

Many parent-child relationships are very positive. The mourner has lost a beloved mother or father. One daughter told me, "I was devastated when my mother died. It's twenty-three years and not a day goes by that she isn't in my thoughts and my heart."

You can safely say to someone like that, "Although I never had the pleasure of meeting your mother, I know how devoted you were and how close you felt to her. I can appreciate how much you will miss her."

A patient wrote this note to his physician, who, he knew, adored his elderly mother:

Dear Dr. ———,

Susan and I both were sorry to hear about your mother's death. We extend our heartfelt sympathy.

I remember chatting with your Mom one day when she dropped in at your office. She had spark and grace. No wonder you spoke of her as a remarkable woman. We want you to know that our thoughts are with you.

Sincerely,

Acknowledge a Painful Relationship

If there were deep conflicts between parent and child, mingled feelings of love and hate are common in the bereaved. The person is likely to have great emotional difficulty in dealing with the death. There may be regret about not working harder to heal rifts or unexpressed resentment that makes it difficult to feel loss.

If a divorced father has died, there may be ambivalent feelings about him—especially if he remarried and had another family and/or was unsupportive to the child. You don't say, "The so-and-so died." But if you're close to the person, you can gently acknowledge the situation by writing something like:

Dear ——,

I'm sad to learn that your father died. I know what a complex situation this is. I look forward to spending some time with you soon. If you'd like to, maybe we can talk about it.

With sincere sympathy,

Share What the Parent Said about the Mourner

We all want to know we pleased our parent. That's why you make an enormous impact when you write to someone, "Your father was so proud of you," and relate specifics that were told to you. A college professor appreciated these words from his dad's colleague: "Your father felt such pleasure in you. At our monthly meetings he'd always bring us up-to-date on your latest research project and which universities were trying to woo you away. He'd talk about your E-mails back and forth arguing politics. He enjoyed them so."

This technique can even change the direction of a life. Someone wrote a condolence note for the first time when the father of her best friend died. There were four children in the family, all in or recently graduated from college. The youngest was a freshman, who was thinking of dropping out of school. The friend wrote to the family:

> *Dear Mrs. Smith, Barbara, Bill, Lisa, and Tony,*
>
> *It's hard to find words to express my sorrow about Mr. Smith. I can't imagine the shock of this loss.*
>
> *I know how proud he was of his family—that Barbara has graduated, that Bill has launched a business career, that Lisa is finishing school next year, and that Tony will study computer science. His children's education was so important to him.*
>
> *Please accept my condolences. I am thinking of you all at this sad time.*

She later learned that her note reminded the son of his father's hopes and values. It influenced the boy to stay in school.

An alcoholic mother died at fifty-two, leaving a twenty-five-year-old daughter. The latter received this note from the mom of her childhood friend:

> *Dear ———,*
>
> *I'm very sad to hear of your mother's death. She and I spent a lot of hours together when you were growing up. I remember the times we carpooled. She made up the schedule for gymnastics classes and it really worked. Your mother truly loved you. I saw the parenting she did. I'll miss her friendship. I send my sincere condolences.*
>
> *Love,*

Here, the writer was in a unique position to give a precious gift to the daughter: assurance that her mother really did love her, despite many painful times over the years.

When her best friend died, leaving two twenty-something daughters, a woman wrote to the bereaved:

Dearest —— and ——,

Please accept my deep and sincere condolences. Your mom's death is such a loss. She so treasured her children above all else. You were her constant sources of pride and joy. She "lit up" each time she spoke of each of you.

I still cannot believe my longtime cherished friend has gone. How I will miss her refreshing spirit, easy wit, laughter, and wonderful conversation. She and I solved the world's problems many times over. She enriched my life like no other, and I will miss her always.

Please know that I grieve with you all. I send my love.

Best,

You can even mention something like "Your father always kept your picture in his wallet. He'd welcome any excuse to pull it out and show it around. You were his joy."

If You Didn't Know the Parent, Focus on the Bereaved

You can concentrate on the grieving son or daughter. An associate wrote this note to a psychologist active in philanthropy, who had lost his ninety-four-year-old father.

> *Dear ———,*
>
> *I was sorry to hear that your father died. I just got the news. Although I never knew him, I do know all about you—and your contributions to the arts and educational communities. Your father raised a son who serves on four boards. I also know that you were a devoted son.*
>
> *I hope that fond memories of him bring you strength and solace.*

In another case, the newspaper carried condolence notices from organizations in which the bereaved was involved. A neighbor used the information in his note:

> *Dear ———,*
>
> *I send condolences on the death of your mother. She was always bragging about you, and would have been thrilled to see all the salutes to her placed by the institutions close to your heart.*
>
> *You are in my thoughts.*
>
> *Warmly,*

Mention the Devotion of the Mourner, if You're Sure of It

One man was a particularly loving son to his elderly mother. He maintained an apartment for her, saw that she was well cared for, and made sure *his* son was attentive to her. When she died at ninety, it was an expected death, but the son was bereft.

This man's daughter-in-law's father, with whom he had often socialized, wrote to him: "I empathize with you, having been there with my own mother. You, like me, are able to say there were no 'shoulda's.' You did all the right things." The bereaved had fulfilled his duty as a son and his mother knew he truly cared about her. He appreciated the note, telling the writer, "I hadn't thought of it that way, but you're right."

I wrote to a business-connected friend on the death of his eighty-eight-year-old mother, a delightful woman whom I had met several times. My note read:

> *Dear ——,*
>
> *I'm sad to hear about your mother's death. She was a dear lady and a model for us all. She had such verve and style. She also had a devoted son in you. We saw how you loved her and took her into your home.*
>
> *We'll miss her, too. We send our sincere condolences.*
>
> *Best,*

For one daughter, taking care of her father while he was dying was an unexpectedly positive experience. "We had never been really close," she told me. "Somehow helping him at the end allowed me to get to know him in a way I hadn't before."

If she was a close friend, I might write something like "I know that you took a sabbatical to care for him and how much that special time meant to you."

If the bereaved shouldered heavy caregiving responsibilities for a very long time and watched the parent suffer, he or she often feels relieved by the death. This is another time to avoid talking about "how grief-stricken you must be." Concentrate instead on the years of care the person provided.

When Death Ends Suffering

One woman had to write to a friend whose mother died of Alzheimer's after years of struggle for all concerned. This woman refused to say she was sorry about the death because it was, in fact, welcomed. True to herself, she wrote, "The last six years have been so difficult for all of you. I also know how hard you tried to do your best for your mother. Remember I am here for you."

Suicide has increased among the elderly and you may have to write to the grieving adult child. You might try something like this, if you're close:

> *Dear ———,*
>
> *I am terribly sorry to hear of your mother's death. I remember you talking of how she wanted to*

die—and how helpless you felt to talk her out of
it. Her mind was made up.

I know how much you loved her. You did every-
thing you could. You have my deepest sympathy.

Or you might quote the suicide note left by
George Eastman, founder of Kodak: "My work is
done, why wait?" You could then recall the mourner's
comments about how special her mother was, and close
with, "I can't imagine what it's like to lose a parent in
this way. I'm thinking of you."

Mention the Struggle

Let's say the mother of your son's friend dies after a
long siege with cancer. You feel a special connection to
the bereaved because you've known him since kindergarten. One woman wrote:

Dear ———,

*I was saddened to hear of your mother's death. I
know how hard these last months have been for
your family—for your mother in her suffering and
for you having to witness it.*

*When I last saw your mother, we spoke and she
was so proud of you. I know you had some good
moments during these last months whose memory, I
hope, will help sustain you.*

Love,

Sometimes the most meaningful notes can come
from someone you don't know very well. When my

father died, I was especially touched by a note from the sister of an in-law. Although she was a very casual acquaintance, she knew the details of my father's illness. She was aware of the distress my family experienced as he slowly died of heart failure. She wrote:

Dear ——,

I was so sorry to hear of your dad's death. I know the last year was a great struggle for him, as it was for your family.

Jerry joins me in sending his sympathy to you and your family.

Fondly,

Mention the Surviving Parent

Is there a surviving elderly parent to worry about? This places an extra burden on the bereaved. One woman told me, "I felt my father's death was anticlimactic. He was in intensive care so often over the years that I'd said good-bye to him ten times before. The main focus was my mother, who was left. Would she disintegrate? Where would she live and in what kind of setting? Would there be enough money to get her taken care of? I was scared to death."

A dear old friend who knew the family very well reflected some of this in her note:

Dearest ———,

I was so sorry to hear about your father. Please accept my deep sympathy. I hope as time goes by you'll be able to remember only the good times and not the stress of the last few years.

How is your Mom taking it? It can't be easy to have to make decisions about her. My heart goes out to you. I had a really difficult time coping with the fact that no matter what I did, it couldn't make things easier and less painful for my mother, or persuade my father to have a happier outlook on life. There's not so much you can do to alter the direction of someone else's life, except your children's . . . and they would prefer you didn't.

I'll keep in touch by mail or phone. Stay well and give my best to your family.

Love,

This was a case where the sharing of a common experience was helpful. The writer even made the bereaved smile with her line (so true) about children.

Someone added this message to a condolence card for a coworker:

Dear ———,

Just wanted to beam some good thoughts your way. I was so sorry to hear about your father. I know you're really busy running back and forth to your mother's house. Let me know if I can cover any of your accounts during this difficult time. Take care.

Other Devices

The best condolence notes tell the bereaved something about the person they may not have known. "I try to give one extra good memory," says a sales manager. "Sometimes it can lighten their load a bit. They may even smile through their tears." This man often frequented a neighborhood camera store over the years and forged a strong bond with the owner. When the owner died at seventy-six, the sales manager wrote to the son:

> *Dear ——,*
>
> *I was a customer of your dad's and knew him really well. I loved going into his store to hear him talk about the old movie stars (like Jean Arthur) and about the big bands.*
>
> *I remember once telling him my favorite song was "I Can't Get Started With You." All of a sudden, he started singing the whole song. I'll never forget it. I loved the moment. What is life but a lot of little moments.*
>
> *I'm sorry for your loss and send my condolences. I will miss your dad.*
>
> *Sincerely,*

Using Imagery

A travel agent felt shocked when her father died. She told me, "A coronary took him, quick. He was perfectly healthy in all of his eighty-four years." An acquaintance wrote:

Dear ———,

I'd like to extend my condolences to you and your family. Losing a parent is so difficult. Perhaps with the arrival of spring the healing process will begin.

Best,

Because the process of grieving is very difficult work, "healing" is a wonderful, quiet image. Healing is also a natural process and does lead to being whole again. Images from nature work, too, because nature involves cycles: winter looks like death; spring looks like new beginnings. But these images must be appropriate to the individual recipient and natural to the person writing about them, or they'll sound awkward.

Did the Deceased Make an Impact on Your Life?

If so, talk about it, as in, "Your father took me fishing for the first time in my life" or, "Your mother introduced me to the ballet." A teacher wrote this note to the daughter of her next-door neighbor, who died of lung cancer at seventy-five:

Dear ———,

I'm deeply sorry to hear about your father. I lived right next door to him. I will miss him so much.

He always gave me a hard time—he loved to tease me. But he was wonderful, often helping me with projects for my art class. He even loaned me his

truck to pick up wood for one project. I'll always
remember him.

With deep sympathy,

A lawyer wrote to a colleague's son:

Dear ——,

*I was saddened to learn that your father passed
away. Joe was one of the people who shaped this
practice and gave it dignity.*

*I recall many times sitting at Bar meetings, bored
with the discussion; then, Dad would rise and
everyone listened. (All I knew was that I did not
want to become the subject of his oratory.)*

*I will always remember him with great fondness.
Please convey my sympathy to Joan and your
family.*

Warmly,

Death of a Spouse or Life Partner

I lost my best friend when my husband died. There was no one I could talk to like I could talk to him. His death was a shock even though he was in and out of the hospital for three years. You get accustomed to living like that—to the fact that there are things you can't do because he's sick. Yet you don't think he'll actually die.

—Widow wed sixty-two years

When a spouse dies, the survivor's world is changed forever. It's a life crisis with multiple losses: a companion, friend, and lover is gone. So is the marriage, possibly financial security, and the couples lifestyle. The survivor is no longer part of a pair; there is no one with whom to share social life and the joys and disappointments of children. A widow (no longer a wife) is deprived of not only a role, but often social status. Widowers can feel lost. For all these reasons and more, gestures that show you care mean a lot.

Certain approaches can help you write words that are real and personal to someone who has lost a mate. Try these suggestions to stimulate your thoughts.

Talk About What Made the Spouse Special

You can provide your own unique perspective, which the mourner wants to hear. Consider this note received by a grieving husband who lost his wife of forty years after a long battle with leukemia. Her best friend wrote:

> *Dear ——,*
>
> *I am filled with sorrow at your enormous loss. I know there are no words that can take away your pain, but I want you to know how much I adored Ginny and her zest for life.*
>
> *She referred to herself as the Eveready Bunny . . . she just kept on going. She was twenty years older than me, but I never thought of her as anything but my contemporary. She always had such zip, which she retained until the very end. On my last visit with her, she gave me a bag of vitamins for my health problems. Even then she was still trying to fix me. Such a woman! Please know that I am here if you want to talk or simply don't want to be alone. I'll give you a call next week.*
>
> *With sincere sympathy,*

A businessman wrote to a fellow church member who had lost her husband:

Dear —————,

I was sorry to hear that Bill had passed away. We served on two committees together. I always admired his integrity, his gift for sharp insight, and his commitment to the congregation and the community. In my experience, he was also a compassionate man who was always the first to lend a helping hand.

He will be missed by all who knew him. Please accept my condolences.

Sincerely,

When his doctor, who had become a personal friend, died of heart disease at fifty-eight, a lawyer wrote to the widow:

Dear Rose,

Sandy and I are so very sorry to hear about Harry's death. Please accept our heartfelt condolences. We don't know what we will do without him. We started out in a patient-doctor relationship, yet it grew to be much more than that. We seemed to have so much in common.

They don't make doctors like Harry anymore. His kind of compassion and humanity was always in short supply, but is even rarer now. He was an original.

Rose, we want you to know we appreciate the friendship of you both. We don't always know

*what to do for you, what is best, what can be truly
helpful. Know that we are here for you, whatever
you need. We'll call you in a few days.*

By using childhood memories, one woman tried to
re-create what the deceased was like in her life. When
her favorite uncle died, she wrote to her aunt and
cousins: "I could always come to Uncle Pete. When I
was a child I could sit on his lap and he would make me
feel loved and accepted. In many ways, he was an extra
father to me."

A woman wrote to the widow of her cousin, who
had died of lung cancer:

Dear ———,

*I'm so sad to hear of Brad's death. Even though
we all knew it was coming, the reality is a shock.
The feeling is "How can it be?" for someone so
full of life.*

*I adored Brad throughout my childhood. He had
those movie star looks and I thought he was the
handsomest and most dashing of men. He was so
much fun, too, a man who loved to have a good
time. Even when I visited him last—and it was
evident he didn't have long—he had jokes to tell.*

*I can't imagine how difficult these last months
have been. Brad was so lucky to have you there
with him. The family just won't be the same without him. I'll remember him always.*

Love,

A colleague or coworker can present a side of the
deceased that the bereaved wouldn't ordinarily see.

One note read,

I extend my deepest condolences at the death of your husband. Ken was a unique man, someone who knew how to manage people and had the patience and intelligence to do it well. I had five bosses last year and it was really rough. Ken was the one who showed me the ropes. Nobody else was willing to take the time—but he did.

I'll always remember him and his kindness.

Sincerely,

This is the kind of note the bereaved will read again and again.

When his partner died, an architect wrote to the widow: "I can only celebrate the man I knew, his character and leadership and decency at a time when these are rare commodities, his wisdom and exuberance for life. Ralph was more than my business partner; he was my dear trusted friend. I—and everyone else at the firm—will miss him."

An accountant wrote an associate:

Dear ———,

I am sorry to hear the sad news about your wife, Sue. I extend my deep sympathy.

I recall meeting Sue for the first time at the Christmas party last year. She was a beautiful, gracious lady who immediately made me feel at ease.

Remember that your friends and colleagues care
about you—and that includes me.

Sincerely,

Reflect on the Couple

You can mention the qualities you most admired in the marriage, as in "In the age of divorce, it was always a treat to watch the two of you together. You laughed a lot and accepted each other. You were so compatible." You can also refer to children left behind, as in "Lewis's wonderful spirit lives in those two little girls," or "You raised two terrific boys together." To know that makes for a constant living memory of the spouse.

During her teen years, one woman baby-sat many Saturday nights for a family in her neighborhood. Twenty years later, when the husband died, she wrote to the widow:

> *Dear Mrs. ——,*
>
> *I truly was saddened to hear of your dear hus-*
> *band's death. I've always thought of you both as*
> *such a warm and spirited couple. It was always a*
> *pleasure to be in your company (even as a disgrun-*
> *tled teenager!).*
>
> *I send my deep and sincere sympathy to you and*
> *yours. I will always remember Mr. —— as a most*
> *charming gentleman—truly a class act.*
>
> *Fondly,*

If you knew the couple well, talk about the mate's positive impact on the survivor. Be specific as in, "Joe was your strongest supporter. I remember that he was the one who encouraged you to get your law degree after you became a paralegal. He knew you had the stuff to do it." This kind of specific reminder can help the bereaved feel their spouse is still an active part of their life in a very tangible way.

One way to handle the death of a spouse you disliked: focus on the mates' relationship with each other, rather than on your feelings. A woman who despised a friend's husband remained true to herself by writing:

Dear ——,

I'm sorry to hear about Henry. I know what difficult times you've been through because I've been aware of them. I also know that you loved him and how much you'll miss him. But most of all I truly know that he loved you deeply.

If you need me, I'm there. I love you.

Beware of Assumptions

You can't predict how people will react when a spouse dies, and any statement that presupposes there is a right way to feel can be very alienating to the bereaved. We tend to believe that the survivor will be devastated, but feelings can run the gamut of sorrow, confusion, disorientation, apathy, guilt, and anger at being abandoned. That's why it's critical to avoid statements like "You must feel sad (or crushed)." Someone who nursed a spouse with Alzheimer's disease for years may now feel a sense of calm and freedom. Or there may be relief that the ordeal is over for both of them and guilt at that relief. There can be grief not only for the death but for what was lost in the relationship due to the illness.

Not All Marriages Are Happy

Don't just assume the marriage was a loving one; not all are. Unless you're sure of the situation, skip phrases like "your beloved Jean (or Andy)" or statements such as "You were the perfect couple."

When a marriage was troubled, the survivor often experiences ambivalent feelings, such as love and anger. Some people feel guilty for failing to work things out with the spouse. If you are close to the bereaved, you might write something like:

> *Dear ——,*
>
> *I'm deeply sorry about Ed's death. I want you to know that I am thinking about you and here for you.*
>
> *I'm sure you have many mixed feelings at this time. I'll call in a few days to see how you are holding up. If you feel like talking, I'm a good listener and at your service.*
>
> *Love,*

If the Marriage Was Truly Unhappy

The most complicated notes involve situations where the deceased ignored the survivor's feelings, was unfaithful, abusive, or self-destructive. There is a tendency to idealize the person who has died and forget shortcomings, so avoid recalling how cheap Clyde was or how Carol gambled away the food money. Then what *do* you write? If you don't know the bereaved well, stick to a general "I'm sorry to hear of ———'s death. You are in my thoughts."

On the other hand, if you're close to the bereaved, death can be viewed as the termination of a stressor. One husband demeaned his wife throughout their marriage and finally tried to shoot her. When he died, the wife received this frank note from her best friend: "Now you have your life before you. Think about what you would like to do that you've never been able to." Says the friend, "She wrote back that she wanted to drive a car without him yelling how stupid she was. She wound up buying her own car and driving all over the state. Now she is trying to find the courage to drive to Colorado. In time I believe she will."

Look at the Stage of Life

A spouse's death at any time turns life upside down for the survivor and involves enormous loss. But there are different things you can say depending on the deceased's age.

Elderly widows and widowers deserve special attention because they are suffering many losses now. Health is in decline; friends and siblings are dying. The loss of a spouse may be just the latest in a whole string of traumas. In this case, you can honestly write, "I can't imagine what a blow it is to lose Jim."

Notes to older people can also refer to the grandparenting role. You can write something like "Charley was such a devoted grandfather," or "I wish Charley had lived to see his new grandchild."

One husband died right after his wife gave birth to their first child. She recalls, "The notes that helped most were those in which the person spoke out loud of the terrible reality of it all and didn't try to cheer me up." A condolence which acknowledged that a tragedy occurred said,

> *Dear ——,*
>
> *I can't find the words to convey my sorrow at Don's death. This is such a horror and so unfair. He was thrilled and proud to be a new daddy. He was crazy about little Jenny. I can't conceive of what you must be going through.*
>
> *I know you're going to need help and I'll call later in the week to see what I can do.*
>
> *Love,*

When an Ex-Spouse Has Died

There are variables to consider in whether (and what) you write to the survivor. The death of an ex arouses all kinds of feelings, depending on the nature of the post-marital relationship. If they were locked in combat or the deceased remarried, the survivor might feel angry. Other issues include: Was the spouse good to the kids? Were the support payments forthcoming (and on time)?

When her ex-husband died accidentally at forty-two, one woman's first reaction was, "Oh boy, where is the money for the kids coming from now? What will happen to my children?" There also may be guilty feelings, such as, "Maybe if I had been more understanding about his long hours, our marriage wouldn't have ended."

If the pair got along well, the ex's death is almost like the death of a spouse. You might write something like,

Dear ———,

I'm sad to hear about Patty's death. Even though you parted, I know you remained close. I've always admired your ability to manage a positive relationship.

I realize how difficult this may be for you. I'll call in a few days to see if you want to talk.

If the relationship was a poor one, I wouldn't write, unless I was an intimate of the survivor. Then I might try something like "I was shocked to hear about Stan's death. I'd love to talk to you when you're up to it." Or "I hope the kids are holding up. Please call me when you're in the mood." People need the support.

On the other hand, someone asked her best friend whose very abusive ex was dying, "What would you want to hear in a condolence message?" She replied, "If I didn't get a note from you telling me to be glad he is out of the picture, I'd be disappointed in you."

When a Significant Other or Companion Has Died

Couples who live together, without marriage, have become more common and you may find yourself writing to a surviving significant other, rather than to a spouse. In this case, you can focus on the life they shared together, how compatible they were, and how happy they made each other. If they got together in midlife, you can say something like "You chose each other at a time of life when you were no longer kids. You knew who you were and what you wanted. It is so cruel that she has been ripped out of your life." If the deceased had children, you can refer to them.

It's always a good idea to try to say something about how special the mourner is, as in "Jim was very lucky to have you through the good years and these last painful ones."

In the case of a gay couple, you can talk about most of the same things to a companion that you would to a spouse. Acknowledge that the two shared an important primary relationship and were a legitimate couple. In one case, the pair had been together for eighteen years. When one partner died of an aneurysm, a relative wrote to the survivor:

Dear ——,

Arnold's death is such a loss. I'm so very sorry. I know how much he meant to you. You were soulmates. You built a wonderful home and shared a beautiful life together.

*He was important to us all. He was there every
Christmas—just as you were. I and the entire family will miss him.*

Or you might try, "Not everyone is fortunate
enough to share a life in such a compatible relationship.
It will be very hard without Jane. You did so many
things together for so many years. I want you to know
we are here for you. We will call you to see if you
feel like talking. We'd like to get together when you
are ready."

An administrator wrote:

Dear ———,

*I am writing to express my deep sorrow at the loss
of your friend and companion Joe. The love and
esteem in which you held each other was apparent
to everyone.*

*You used to say that the important thing in a rela-
tionship is that people should respect and admire
each other and share the same value system. You
two had it all. I'm thinking of you.*

Warmly,

Following Up with
Meaningful Gestures

Once you've sent your note, you're not off the hook
entirely. If you promised support or assistance, follow
up with a concrete offer.

Try to be sensitive and realize that the bereaved is

likely to be lonely. One woman received a most poignant response from a friend. The person walked up to her, pressed a key into her hand, and said, "You know there were nights when I felt I just could not go home and face an empty house at night." Left unspoken was the message, "If you feel that way, don't go home; come to me." The widow never used the key, but it hung in her kitchen, almost like a talisman. When she remarried, the hardest thing for her to do was to return the key.

Be proactive and say, "Let's go to the movies (or the museum) or out for dinner." Take the person away for the weekend. Come up with ideas, and don't be put off by a "no." People sometimes become very depressed at first and don't want to go out and do things. But keep inviting them.

When someone asked a retired widower to lunch about a month after his wife's death, he was grateful. Over a leisurely meal, he talked about the good times and his wife's contribution as a member of the zoning board. He felt better getting out and being with people.

Widowers may be totally unprepared for being alone. They may have relied on their wives as their only confidantes and as guardians of their social life. A little kindness goes a long way.

Many widows find they don't fit in when their husbands die and they are no longer part of a couple. They are sometimes dropped by married friends just when they need social support. Men may have the same problem, although an extra man is usually more welcome at someone's dinner party than an extra woman.

It is usually helpful, too, for widows to hear from other widows about their own experiences, how severe their pain was, how it changed over time to something that felt bearable. There tends to be immediate rapport and understanding. Usually the person says something like "My heart goes out to you. I lost my husband last year and I think I know something about what you are feeling."

And throughout the year, you can continue your support. Be thoughtful on holidays. Someone sent a Christmas card to a widow, adding a handwritten, "This first Christmas without —— must be a very difficult one for you. I just want you to know I'm thinking of you."

Other kinds of help are valuable for a widow, too, especially an older woman. She can no longer call on her husband to hang pictures, fix the faucet, or deal with financial details. Help with tax returns would likely be appreciated. One elderly widow who didn't drive a car found her world shrinking because of lack of transportation. Her husband had chauffered her everywhere. Lifts to go shopping or attend meetings or religious services can make a tremendous difference.

Death of a Child

Is there a greater loss or agony for a family than the death of a child? "It's as if part of your body has been torn away," says a mother who still grieves. "Nothing in life prepares you for it."

No matter what words you use when responding to the death, as a bystander, you're going to feel them lacking compared to the enormity of the loss. Don't let feelings of helplessness, hopelessness, and discomfort stop you from doing what is right.

When communicating with the grieving parents, accept that they may be inconsolable. They may be consumed with guilt that they didn't love or protect the child enough or treated the child insensitively at times. "If only (I hadn't given him the keys to the car, or I'd recognized the symptoms earlier)" is a common theme.

What can you really say that will make a difference? Probably very little—but that little bit is very important. Here's how to write something genuine and meaningful.

Consider the Age of the Child

It's unnatural to outlive a son or daughter, regardless of age. But what you write when an adult child has died will differ from the approach for the death of a toddler. In the first instance, the person didn't live a complete life span; in the second, the child barely got to live at all. The parents' grief is immense in both cases, but when death occurs before adulthood, along with the loss comes the death of all hopes and dreams for the future of this child.

If the Child Was Very Young

In this case, there isn't much to write about. You can't refer to many memories or a past history. But if you did know the parent well, you might say something like "I can't imagine the sadness that Lily is no longer in your life. Little as she was, she made an impact. I hope you can remember the joy and love she brought." These are words of comfort.

When a six-year-old or a teenager has died, there are all those unrealized possibilities. A note expressing sympathy for the death of a high school or college student might mention the potential unfulfilled, as in, "She had her whole life ahead of her. It's just so hard to believe this could happen. I'm thinking of you at this terrible time."

For Grown Children

Some people think it is easier to lose an adult child; it is not. So much has been invested emotionally in the person. Because the relationship has had a chance to fully develop, the parent may be losing a friend as well as a son or daughter. As a mother explained, "A young child isn't formed yet. My son was an adult. He lived in another state, but he'd call me from his car at the drop of a hat. He was so much fun."

In such a case, a note like this one from a casual friend can mean a lot:

> Dear —— and ——,
>
> *I was profoundly sorry to hear about Mitchell's death. I know how close you were. I extend my heart and my hand to you and your family at this time of sorrow.*
>
> *Lovingly,*

Consider the Circumstances

Was it a sudden death—an accident or suicide—or was illness the cause? Regardless, the best thing to do is listen to your honest reactions and express them.

One mother lost a thirty-year-old son after a battle with a rare disease. Among the most touching notes she received were those from others who had suffered very similar losses, including this one:

> Dear ——,
>
> *My son died last year of heart problems that plagued him for years. He was the joy of my life. I know that there are no words to lessen your sorrow. We bring our children up to let them go, but not so completely or so soon.*
>
> *Please know you are in my thoughts.*

Someone else who had lost a grown daughter wrote:

Dear ——,

I am so sorry for this nightmare. For myself, I have found that the hole remains always in my heart. Oddly enough, one of the few comforts is the time I spend in the great outdoors. As the seasons change, they symbolize the circle of life—the world dies and then lives again. Walking a country road or watching the waves at the shore seems to have the power of healing.

Perhaps my experience will have some meaning for you.

The recipient told me, "The idea that she'd write such a beautiful letter was so very touching. I was extremely depressed at the time. Her words *did* help."

An attorney wrote to a colleague and his wife, whose eighteen-year-old daughter died in an automobile accident on the way to the prom:

Dear —— and ——,

Having just hung up the phone, I am sitting here unable to focus. Hearing about Sally's death leaves me shocked and numb. This is every parent's worst bad dream.

Although I never met Sally, I clearly remember you speaking of her and her accomplishments with great pride. I can't imagine a greater loss. Jean and I want you to know that you are in our thoughts and prayers.

With deepest sympathy,

The following note expresses sadness for a life ended too soon. It was written to the father of a twenty-five-year-old dancer who died in a skiing accident:

Dear Mr. ———,

I sink in sorrow at the news of Joyce's death. So much in life is unfair, yet this is too untimely, too cruel.

I worked with Joyce and she was a good friend to me. When I think of her, I think of sunshine. Her smile brightened the lives of all who knew her and worked with her. She had such sparkle and intelligence. I join in your grief. Please accept my condolences.

Sincerely,

Unfortunately, losing a child to suicide is more common than we realize. Suicide is the third leading cause of death (after injury and homicide) for young people fifteen to twenty-four years of age. Here you want to acknowledge that this is not an ordinary death; a special tragedy has occurred. Furthermore, a child's suicide confronts the bereaved's validity as a parent. Since suicide is an unnecessary death, parents not only blame themselves, they often feel rage at the child for doing such a thing. Someone wrote:

Dear ——— and ———,

I cannot conceive of your heartache at this tragic moment. I can only remember Jim's handsome, smiling face at your anniversary dinner. He was bouncing with positive energy and so happy about the dramatics award he'd won. We joked about his having the family gene for showmanship.

I had a soft spot for Jim. I admired his spunk and especially his sweetness. I'll always, always remember him. I am so sorry for this nightmare. I can only hope that someday you can find some sort of peace.

All my love and deepest sympathy,

You can also write, "I don't know what to say to you. You are in my thoughts and my heart." Because a child's suicide is so tragic, support is especially important. If you really care about the parents, add, "I'll call you" and then make sure to follow up on it.

Mention Memories and Qualities

When you write, "We have wonderful memories of ——," that says, "I'm remembering the best of this child." Someone wrote this note to the parents of her husband's childhood friend:

Dear Mr. & Mrs. ——,

We share your sorrow and send our deepest condolences to you and your family.

We have beautiful memories of Matthew. His zest for life, devotion to family, and adoration of his children were remarkable. Gordon's voice always fills with warmth and joy when he recalls their years together. The old neighborhood, boys raised as family who faced adulthood, marriage and parenthood together.

Matthew is in our prayers every night as you are in our thoughts in the days and months ahead.

With deep affection,

A niece wrote:

Dear Aunt —— and Uncle ——,

I've written this letter three times and haven't been able to finish it. The sadness and loss is still so overwhelming. I can't help but believe that such a strong spirit as Sean's will be with us forever. His bravery during these past few months will inspire me for the rest of my life.

It is a tribute to Sean that he made such wonderful memories for everyone he touched. The bonds he formed with his cousins and friends are the truest and most enduring I've ever seen. And the love and loyalty he had for you and his children will never die. I know he'll stay a part of each and every one of the people he cherished forever.

Of course I only see that face with a big smile and my favorite sense of humor of all time. The highest compliment we ever paid each other was to admit that it would be dangerous for us to live in the same city. I wish we had the chance. Your strength and support and unwavering faith have been inspirational. You are in my prayers.

Love,

Consider this note to the parent of a ten-year-old nephew:

Dear ——,

As I write to you, I sit with my photo album, looking at pictures of Colin at Little League, at the shore last summer when he was the beach ball king, and at Thanksgiving dinner. He was so vibrant, he never sat still—and those wonderful freckles. He is alive in my heart.

Mention the Parents' Efforts

If the child struggled with a long illness or with an addiction or behavior problem, and the parents tried valiantly to save him or her, you can refer to that, as in this note:

Dear —— and ——,

I cry as I write to you, for what heartbreak can possibly surpass what you are going through.

Since last year, both of you have fought so tenaciously to get the best treatments, the best doctors, the best hospital for Eleanor. I have marveled at your strength and courage. You did everything humanly possible.

My love is with you.

Talk About the Funeral

This is an option especially when you don't know the family well. You can mention the numbers of people who attended and what that turnout reflected. One note, written after condolences had been expressed over the phone, did it this way:

> Dear ——,
>
> You are always on my mind, as is the experience of Brendan's funeral. So many people pouring out their love and regard for him, and for your entire family. It was unforgettable.
>
> May you draw strength always from loving memories of him, and from the countless friends who care about you.
>
> Warmly,

Miscarriage and Stillbirth

Parents can feel desolate after a miscarriage or stillbirth, experiencing intense guilt and pain and wondering whether things would have been different if they'd gone to the doctor sooner or gotten more rest.

Miscarriage is a significant loss, whether it occurs at seven weeks into the pregnancy or at twenty weeks. It's important, if you're close to the couple, to say how sorry you are and acknowledge your acceptance that this loss is real to them, as in:

Dear —— and ——,

I'm truly sad to hear about the miscarriage. I know this child meant so much to you. I want both of you to know I'm thinking of you at this difficult time.

With love,

Stillbirth involves exquisite emotional pain because there has been a pregnancy and birth. The crib and baby clothes are ready and other preparations have been made. The mother also often feels sad because although she knew the baby was "real"—she felt it doing somersaults inside her belly—others in her life can't realize the significance of what she has lost because they didn't have the chance to develop a relationship with her baby.

When a joyful event ends in tragedy, you want to acknowledge that, as in:

Dear —— and ——,

I can't imagine what heartbreak you are going through after all those months of hope and anticipation. I want you to know I care and am thinking of you. I'll call to find out if there's anything I can do.

With sincere condolences,

Never tell parents who have had a stillbirth or miscarriage, "You can have other children." That has nothing to do with the fact that a loss has occurred. Don't remind a woman that she "wasn't very far along." Her hopes and dreams for the baby began the moment she found out that she was pregnant. Skip "At

least you didn't have a chance to get to know the baby."
Realize, too, that men may be hurting in these cases.
They're sometimes shut out of condolences, but they
need to hear them.

Loss of a Grandchild

Grandparents are doubly crushed when a grandchild
dies. There is not only the loss of a grandchild, but
they must also witness the suffering of their own
children.

A neighbor wrote this note to an elderly woman
she knew well:

> *Dear Mrs. ———,*
>
> *I'm so sad to hear the news of your grandson's
> death. It was only last week that I saw him visiting
> you. It was obvious that he loved you very much. I
> cannot imagine your pain at losing him so young.
> He had so much before him.*
>
> *My thoughts are with you and your daughter and
> son-in-law.*
>
> *Respectfully,*

For a grandmother who had experienced many
losses in her life, her granddaughter's death was the
latest blow. This note to her came from a family friend:
"As the days go by, I think of you often and how much
you've gone through—too much. Belinda's death is an
unspeakable tragedy. I am so very sorry for this loss."

Loss of a Stepchild

The stepparent and child relationship is very complex. Some people may feel cool or downright hostile toward stepchildren; others have close, loving relationships. Stepparents who have forged strong bonds can feel bereft, yet they may be treated like outsiders.

Unless you know the people well, keep your message very general, as in "I'm so sorry to hear about Jessica's death. My thoughts are with you at this difficult time. With deep sympathy."

A woman who had been close to her stepson received this note from a friend:

> *Dear ——,*
>
> *I'm sorry to hear the sad news about Gerald. You were a second mother to him—and he loved you back. I know he brought joy to your life. You were an asset to his. I send sincerest condolences.*

When writing to the biological parent, be sure to include a loving stepparent in your condolence note, as in, "I'm thinking of you and Janet." And of course you should write separately to both biological parents if you knew the couple well—don't assume your condolences to one will be conveyed to the other.

Following Up

"The opportunity to talk honestly about my feelings was the hardest thing to find when my daughter died," says a woman who lost an eight-year-old. "Nobody wanted to hear about it because they didn't know what to say. The truth is, they didn't need to say anything. They just needed to listen."

Grieving is a long process. If you care about the bereaved, follow up. The greatest gift is to call back in a month and say, "I was just remembering Jeff and how he —————. I wanted to tell you I'm thinking of you." There's a need to know the child lives on, as will happen when people remember.

One mother told me, "When my son died, his English teacher had the kids in his class make a book of anecdotes about their times with him. It was one of the nicest things anyone did."

You can call the bereaved and say, "Let's go for a walk (or out for lunch)." But don't give up on them or be distressed if they decline. It's hard to be with people after your child dies. The parent has to reach a point where he or she can do it. Keep trying. Structure an activity that won't make a demand on the person, as in "I'll pick you up to see the flower show at noon. We'll have a quick lunch and you'll be back in a few hours."

Remember Each Family Member

If an adult child has died (and was married), the surviving spouse, rather than the parents, tends to get most of the attention. Your support for the grieving mom and dad can be extremely welcome. You can talk about the deceased's plans and dreams for the future that will never be realized, as in "He always wanted to go to medical school."

Marking Painful Holidays

Mother's Day or Father's Day can be terribly painful times for parents who have lost a child. If you're close, you might send a note. You don't have to say anything about the child. Just write something like, "I'm thinking of you." The recipient will know why you wrote. Or send flowers or a plant, writing a line on the gift card like "Just want you to know you're in my thoughts."

One woman calls the mother of a friend who died of AIDS on the friend's birthday every year. "I'll say, 'It's Steve's birthday today. We always used to go out and have spaghetti for his birthday.' If we laugh about something, I'll say, 'Steve would have liked that.' It's been twenty years and I haven't forgotten him."

Helping with Tasks

If an unmarried adult child dies, his or her friends, employer, and coworkers must be notified of the death. You can offer to help call people to let them know.

If the cause of death involved stigma (as in AIDS, drugs, alcohol, or suicide), parents often feel guilty that they didn't know or didn't do enough to prevent the death. If you wish, you can say, "I know of (or can get information on) a support group if you're interested." Then back off. Some people will want to take advantage of a group; others will not. The Compassionate Friends, an international support group for families who have experienced the death of a child, is an excellent resource.

Death of a Sibling, Other Relative, or Friend

Although we mark the death of someone else's parent or spouse or child without question, we tend to pay less attention when a sibling dies and to minimize the loss of other relatives and friends even further. Yet these people may have been as important in a life as a mother or a mate. Your acknowledgment that something significantly painful has happened—and that someone may be suffering—means a lot to the bereaved. Here's how to respond sensitively to losses that are frequently discounted.

When a Sister or Brother Dies

The sibling relationship is the longest one we have. Our brothers and sisters are the ones who most closely share our early history. They saw a special part of us, which is why this loss can be traumatic. The surviving sibling can feel forgotten and alone; all the attention may focus on the grieving spouse or parents. Words of condolence should express your concern and support. But before you compose a note, consider the particular sibling relationship.

When the Siblings Were Close

It's easiest to write when the siblings had a loving relationship. Just a few lines can say a lot, as in:

Dear ——,

I'm so sad to hear about Catherine's death. I can't imagine what a blow it is to lose such a devoted sister.

Please accept my sincere condolences. Take care of yourself and remember I'm always here if you want to talk.

You can also say in a note, "When things calm down, let's get together and talk about our memories of your brother." Talking in person can give the sibling a new perspective. He or she may feel, "I never knew that about my brother. It's a dimension I didn't see."

When a successful computer industry executive died of a brain tumor at fifty-nine, his brother received this note from an old friend:

Dear ——,

I cried when I heard about Terry's death. How cruel that the baby of the family should leave us so young. (Today, fifty-nine is young.) He had so

much creativity and vision to offer, so many pro-
jects still to be done. A life yet unfinished.

I am so very sorry. With sincere sympathy,

A man received this note when his brother, a painter, died:

Dear ———,

We are saddened to hear about Paul. His paint-
ing—the landscape we love so much—hangs in
our living room and will always remind us of him.
We remember the day we bought it from him. He
was uncomfortable about selling work to friends
and didn't want to take any money from us. We
finally talked him into a fair price.

That was your brother—fiercely proud, unfail-
ingly generous. Adam and I will miss him always.
We extend our sympathy.

Sincerely,

When her older sister died, one woman's hair turned white overnight. "I lost my best friend," she told me. "She was much more a mother to me than my own mother. She was always there." Eleven years later she still cries when she talks about her sister. "I'll never get over her death," she said.

In such a case, you might write something like:

Dear ———,

I'm deeply sorry to hear about Maureen's death.
You talked of her so often as your "second
mother." I know that she is irreplaceable.

If you care to talk, I'm here for you. Please accept my condolences.

When her brother drowned, a young advertising manager received this note from a relative:

Dear ———,

In all the chaos and despair surrounding Randy's death, it's easy for a sister to get lost. I just want you to know that you are on my mind. I can't conceive of the shock you must be going through.

I know it's a tremendous consolation to your parents that you are here with them. I'm so very sorry for this nightmare. I send my love and deepest sympathies.

A sibling who is the last one left can really feel alone in the world, even if surrounded by family.

An eighty-year-old widow who lost the last of her six siblings received this note from a neighbor who knew the family well:

Dear ———,

I don't know what to say to you. Nora's death is such an enormous loss.

It's hard to picture one of you without the other, or a world without Nora speaking her mind. I will never forget her.

You are not alone. Please let me help at this difficult time. I'll stop by to see what shopping or errands I can take care of for you. I send sincerest condolences.

When the Siblings Weren't Close

Some siblings had a stormy past. The more conflicted the relationship, the harder it is for the survivor to come to grips with the loss—and the more careful you should be when you write.

If you don't know the person well, minimal and neutral is best. What's most touching to the bereaved is the knowledge that you took the time to write. Stick to something like this:

> *Dear ———,*
>
> *I just heard about your brother's death. I'm very sorry.*
>
> *Please know that you are in my thoughts.*
> *With deepest sympathy,*

What if the siblings hadn't spoken to each other in years? If you're close to the survivor, you could really be helpful by referring to the mixed feelings, as in "I just heard about Beth. I'm sorry that she died before you had a chance to sort things out. My heart goes out to you."

Or you can say something like "I know you had rocky times. But you also told me about very happy times when you were younger. I hope you can find comfort in those good memories." If you're not close, just say, "I want you to know I am thinking of you."

Other Family Relationships

All kinds of relatives can be closer than a natural parent or sibling, but you have to know the person well to be aware of that. In these instances, you can talk about the special relationship the person enjoyed with the deceased and the needs it fulfilled.

Someone may have been raised by a grandparent or the latter may have otherwise played a significant role in the person's life. You can refer to that in a note, as in "I remember how your grandfather always took you to the auto shows," or "I always envied that your grandmother took you shopping with her. Once she even took you to get your makeup done. She was *fun*."

A woman who was very close to her late grandmother described the relationship this way: "I spent a lot of time at her house when I was growing up. She was always there to listen or cuddle when you needed it. She and I disagreed on almost everything—religion, politics, philosophy, you name it. It didn't matter, though. She used to tell me that as long as I was a good person and did my best at everything I tried, she couldn't be anything but proud of me. She taught me that you don't have to like everything someone thinks or does to love them completely."

If I had known her when her grandmother died, I might have written:

> *Dear ——,*
>
> *I am so sorry to hear of your grandmother's death. What a terrible loss. Though I never met her, I feel I got to know her through your eyes. She was obvi-*

ously one of those rare people who knew what unconditional love is and gave it always.

I'm sad that you lost someone you could always count on and trust. I send my sincerest condolences.

You can change the focus and talk about what a caring grandchild the bereaved was, as in "Your mother told me so often how you'd visit your grandfather and take him out to lunch. I know he was good to you, but you were also good to him." You may also want to mention, "How are your parents taking this?"

My own aunt Gus was a key figure in my life. I knew she loved me and she always made me feel special. When she died, two close friends called me, but nobody wrote. One reason was the lack of importance others place on such a death. Another is the fact that the word doesn't get out as widely as it does when a parent or spouse dies. I realize now that I would have appreciated words like "You often told me how special she was to you and how accepting. I also know that you brought joy to her life. I remember your taking her out to dinner at a fancy restaurant for her birthday every year. I hope such memories keep her alive in your heart."

One woman felt devastated when her aunt, a surrogate mother and huge presence in her life, died. A close friend wrote to her:

Dear ——,

I'm sad to hear about your Aunt Kate. She was a wonderful person and great lady who taught you well about what is important in this life. May the lessons you learned enhance your experiences in the

years ahead. Then she will always be alive and a
part of you forever.

Another note to a nephew read: "I'm sorry to hear about your uncle's death. I know how close you were to him and that he was like a father to you. I'm sorry you've lost someone who means so much."

When her cousin died in an auto accident, a kindergarten teacher received a condolence card from a family friend, sharing this memory: "Today I recalled the fun you and Laura had jumping rope at all the family Thanksgivings. It didn't matter that you were all dressed up. You loved to keep moving!" The recipient loved it. "I remember . . ." is always a wonderful thing to say.

When her seventeen-year-old niece died, a woman received only one condolence card, from one of her husband's clients, with these simple lines:

Dear ——,

We were truly sorry to hear of the loss of your niece. Our prayers are with you.

This unexpected note, short and sincere, touched her deeply. The spareness is powerful; the simple signature adds to the dignity.

I wrote this note to someone who lost a young nephew, shortly after another death had occurred in the family:

Dear ——,

I just heard today that your little nephew died. We're so very sorry to hear of this latest heartbreak

in a year of heartbreak. We weep at this tragedy
and send our condolences.

Love,

If the bereaved had a poor relationship with the deceased, but *you* liked the person, it is appropriate to say, "I will miss your sister (or aunt or grandmother)" or, "I loved your brother because —————. Here are my recollections of him." Hearing the story might add another perspective.

When a Friend Dies

*You've got something you want to talk about. You
dial the phone—and it's, "My God, she isn't
there." Whom can I call when I have a fight with
my husband? Whom can I crab to about my son's
new girlfriend? Who will understand the way she
does? There is no one else.*

—48-year-old high school teacher on
the death of her best friend

Friends do so much to provide love and safety in life. The friend may have been the person's closest confidant, the one who accepted and understood best. The death of such a friend can be devastating because irreplaceable emotional nourishment has been lost. This can be especially true now that so many of us live far away from family members; often friends fill the gap and are as close as relatives.

Someone who has lost a close friend may feel all of the emotions stirred by the loss of a loved one. Yet our society tends to ignore such a death, offering little or no social support. That's why it's important to extend a hand.

When writing to someone who is hurting, you want to remind the person of how much the friend meant and how much they shared together. Someone who lost an older woman friend received this note:

> Dear ———,
>
> I'm sorry to hear about Peggy's death. You spoke of her so often that I felt I knew her pretty well myself.
>
> She was especially intriguing to me as an early feminist in the New York public school system and someone who always knew who she was. At the same time you talked of her strong self esteem, you spoke of her spirit, commitment, and honesty. "There's nothing wishy-washy about Peggy," you'd often say.
>
> She was obviously one of a kind. I can't imagine how you'll miss her. Remember, I'm here to talk if you want to.
>
> Love,

One woman lost a male friend to AIDS. "We were in our playpens together and close all our lives. I tried to be there for him while he was so ill," she explains. When he died, someone wrote to her:

> Dear ———,
>
> I felt so sad to hear that time finally ran out for Walter. How large his loss to you.

*He was afraid of being forgotten, but I know you
will never forget him. I also remember what a
trooper you were during the worst times and how
you stuck by him from beginning to end.*

*There will never be another friend like him, but
you are a one and only, too. You're the kindest person I know. I'm thinking of you.*

The cancer death of a friend who was exactly the
same age stirred an editor's fear of her own mortality,
plus guilt that she hadn't been available enough while
the person was dying. She appreciated this note from a
close pal:

Dear —————,

*I'm sad to hear Cathy died. Though I only met her
once or twice, I felt I knew her because you talked
of her plight.*

*I know you feel that you let her down and should
have been more attentive. But the fact is, you often
came through for her. Be proud of what you did
do. It was a lot.*

Love,

When another woman's friend died, it meant the
loss of her connection to childhood. "We had our ups
and downs, but we knew each other for twenty-four
years," she mused wistfully. "My parents and sister are
dead. Now she's gone, too." In such a case, I'd try to
anticipate the "aloneness" she might be feeling and
write something like:

Dear ——,

I'm sad to hear the news about Blanche. I know your friendship didn't always run smoothly, but in the end you stuck together. She was a vital piece of your life.

I can't imagine what her loss represents to you, but I want you to know that you are not alone. Your friends care about you—and if you need me, I am here.

Love,

It is especially important to recognize those who lose friends in later life. Friendships have tremendous positive impact on psychological well-being and satisfaction in the elderly. Friends often become closer supports than family when an older woman is widowed. They are companions who share precious memories and provide a sense of continuity as well as practical help to each other. When writing to an older person, you can refer to the good times shared.

An eighty-four-year-old woman who lost a childhood friend received this note from another old friend:

Dear ——,

I felt so terribly sad that Paula died last weekend. I extend my sincerest condolences. Knowing how close the two of you were, I can't imagine how lost you must feel.

I do remember how inseparable you were way back in third grade at P.S. 22 and how your relationship stayed close through both your marriages, your

*children and grandchildren, and even when she
moved to California. It was only a few weeks ago
that we were on the phone—and you said to me,
"Gotta go now. That's Paula long-distance on
call-waiting."*

*May you find comfort in the memories of happy
times together. Let's have lunch and a good cry. I'll
call to set up a date.*

Love,

Older adults are likely to feel very sad and alone if
they outlive all their friends, especially if they have
mobility problems that make it difficult to go out and
make new ones. That's why asking someone you care
about to lunch or tea or to join you in an activity, such
as a bridge club, is the right thing to do. Older people
who have lost friends need to make other connections
so that they can move on with their lives.

Death of a Pet

Our culture doesn't place much value on the relationship between an owner and a pet. Yet when a beloved animal dies, pet owners often feel grief-stricken. A unique relationship has been lost. Because animals can mean so much, it's important to show concern in this situation, as you would if a loved one had died. The pet *is* a loved one.

Because the pet/owner relationship tends to be discounted by others, grieving owners may feel ashamed of being so upset. It helps to reassure them that what they are feeling is normal by saying or writing, "I think I can imagine how you feel" or, "I know other people who have felt the same way you're describing right now when their dogs died."

You can reflect on some experience you've had yourself. A small detail can be helpful, as in "I remember when I lost my cat. I felt sad for weeks." Or, "I had a very hard time going to work the next day. I grieved a long time, but then got back to myself." Someone wrote on a printed card, "I sympathize with you, having lost my own beloved Rags. You are in my prayers."

Here are other ways to acknowledge the loss and offer support to someone you care about.

Respect the Depth of the Relationship

When a pet dies, friends and relatives who really love animals understand what the owner is going through. Those who don't can be astonished at the depth of the pet/owner bond. One woman explains her devotion this way: "The great thing about cats is they don't talk, but they communicate. They're cuddly and such a comfort, so much fun to play with."

This woman was distraught when kidney and heart problems killed her cat. While Taffy was sick, she'd get on the phone with friends and sob, "She's taken a turn for the worse." Another woman spent a thousand dollars on radiation treatments for a cat that had cancer.

"There is no good explanation for the relationships," says a psychologist who runs a hotline for grieving pet owners. "There's a kind of intimacy where even if the owner lives the fullest life, including spouse and children, he or she still has a different relationship with an animal. It's a nonjudgmental relationship."

Pet owners need people to bear witness to their loss. You do that when you write or say, "I'm sorry." A dog owner received this note from a simpatico friend:

Dear ——,

I'm sad to hear about Laddie. His death is an enormous blow, I know. He brought such joy to your life. He followed you around like a shadow. No wonder he was "your baby."

I send my condolences. I'm here for you if you want to talk.

Love,

Realize Animals Aren't Easily Replaced

Resist the urge to compare the death of a dog or cat—or even a goldfish—to another death. You don't want to imply that the loss of an animal is a lesser loss than that of a person. You want to communicate, "I realize this is a terrible experience." Whatever you do, don't try to make the person feel better by pointing out, "You can get another dog." We all say such things because we replace pets all the time; we don't expect them to live more than ten or fifteen years.

There may or may not be another animal in the person's life, but he or she feels the relationship with the lost pet is unique. One does not replace the love of a companion. You can write:

Dear ——,

I'm so sorry about Blossom. I know this was a real loss for you. As much as it hurts, I hope you know you gave her a really good life.

Love,

Actually, virtually anything you'd say to someone who lost a family member is appropriate for a bereaved pet owner. Be honest with yourself, however. If you feel, "It's only a cat," and it's awkward to call a friend —if you think that you won't do a good job—write instead. That's when cards come in handy. You can add a simple handwritten "I'm thinking of you." Or write a stand-alone note, such as:

> Dear ———,
>
> *I'm sad that Blackie died. I know how much you'll miss him. He was an important part of your life. You are in my thoughts.*
>
> *Love,*

Talk About Your Recollections of the Animal

Dogs live the equivalent of about seven years for every "human" year of life. When someone lost a dog after ten years together, a friend sent this note:

> Dear ———,
>
> *I have such lovely memories of Delilah and what a sweet dog she was. I remember how she always loved to sit in your lap on the sofa. She was a lucky one.*
>
> *You were lucky, too, to have her so long. I offer my deepest sympathy.*

Another note read:

Dear ———,

*What can I say. I know how special Bruno was to
you. You called him your best friend. I remember
your bringing him home when he was seven weeks
old. So cute!*

*My condolences on losing this beloved companion.
I'll miss the little guy too.*

Understand the Guilt of Euthanasia

There are special problems when an animal must be euthanized. The owner always feels tremendous guilt. One recalls, "My dog was so sick, I knew I'd have to put her to sleep, but I couldn't bear to think of it. It was the single hardest thing I've ever done."

Although owners agonize over whether it was too soon or it was too late, there is also relief. They had to go out of their way to keep the sick animal going and bear witness to its physical suffering.

Some people get into marathons of self-sacrifice while caring for a sick animal. If conversation is comfortable, you can say something like "You did a beautiful thing by carrying JoJo up the stairs for six months. You cared for him well and now you don't have to do it anymore."

You want to send the message that "Although you're grieving for the animal, your first job is to take care of yourself." This might be a place to say to someone close who is dangerously stressed out, "Here's something that may be of comfort," and give a gift of healing, such as a prepaid massage.

There are also bereavement groups available for pet loss. If you wish, you can mention to a pet owner that you know of such groups. For information, call a local ASPCA (American Society for the Prevention of Cruelty to Animals) or Humane Society. Groups are also available on the Internet. Type in "pet loss."

Funeral Services, Memorial Services, and Other Rituals

Nobody likes funerals or memorial services, but it's important to attend them if you care about the person who has died, or those left behind. Your presence acknowledges that an important life has been lost and conveys your personal support. The bereaved do notice how many people attended, who did or did not show up. If they look back later and find "Nobody from my office (or my bridge club) went to the funeral," they can feel alienated.

If you're struggling with "Should I go or shouldn't I," realize that it's only human to feel anxious about such ceremonies. It's awkward to face the bereaved in person and *say* something. You're also put in touch with your own mortality and the possibility of losing those you love. The information that follows will educate you to various ritual occasions when it's appropriate to "be there" and help you feel a little less uncomfortable, a lot more confident.

Events Preceding the Funeral

Certain rituals allow people to pay their respects to the deceased and the bereaved before the funeral. They take place at the funeral home or (only occasionally today) in the family's home. Although they are essentially the same, they can have somewhat different meanings, depending on the region and family background.

At a *wake* or a *viewing*, the body is usually present. It is *not* present at a *visitation* or *calling hours,* which may be memorial calling hours or a reception for friends and family. These events may be quiet and somber in tone, or not, depending on the personality of the family and the circumstances of death. In certain ethnic groups, a wake may be a spirited affair to distract the bereaved *after* the funeral.

For information on time and location, check the obituary in the newspaper. It may read something like "Friends may call Wednesday, October 1, from 2 to 4 P.M. and 7 to 9 P.M. at Smith Funeral Home, 100 E. 4th Street." Or call the funeral home, or ask a family member. Your visit is an important personal gesture of support. You need only stay for five or ten minutes. There is also a bonus: if you express condolences to the bereaved at this time, you are not required to write a condolence note (although you may wish to do so in some cases, regardless).

Funerals

The purpose of a funeral is to memorialize the loved one and to comfort the bereaved. Funerals, however, also bring comfort to us. They help us feel a sense of community in honoring the dead together. They connect us to the person who has died.

It's always tempting to skip a funeral. We're all busy and there's likely to be something else pressing at the same time. Go anyway. The death of a loved one is one of the most critical life events people can go through, so you want to be there (unless the funeral is private, in which case attendance is limited to those who have been invited by the family.) Do leave young children under age six or so at home.

The funeral service is usually held within a few days of the death and generally indicates the body is present. If the deceased was a practicing Catholic, the service is part of a Mass. When you attend a service for someone of another faith, you are not expected to say or do anything contrary to your own religion.

At some funerals, including Jewish ones, the family is usually present in the chapel thirty minutes to an hour before the service. You can talk to the bereaved then.

Burial or Cremation

We tend to assume that only family and closest friends go to the interment. In fact, it is often appropriate for all guests to be there. After a Jewish funeral, it is considered a good deed to participate in burial of the dead. In northern parts of the United States, winter burials may be delayed due to frozen soil and some cemeteries actually close for the coldest months.

The family may opt for graveside services, rather than a funeral, if they want an abbreviated service, or in cases where travel or traffic conditions make a procession to the cemetery very difficult.

Cremation has also become increasingly common. There may or may not be a service at the crematorium, following the funeral. Ashes may be buried or placed in a building in the cemetery or taken home in an urn and placed on the mantelpiece. Other families scatter the ashes in a lake or other body of water that meant something to the deceased.

Memorial Services

Memorial services, which ordinarily indicate the body is *not* present, have become popular in recent years. The family may choose this option because it is too painful to see the body of someone they love or because the death occurred elsewhere (perhaps even in another country). Or there may *be* no remains, as in the case of a war death.

The service usually takes place within a week of death. Today, however, when some families are dispersed around the globe, the service may be postponed until a holiday (such as Thanksgiving) when family members come together.

A memorial service tends to involve more of an effort to celebrate the person's life, although some funerals today do that too. One service for a man who died comparatively young closed with the song "Singing in the Rain." The deceased, who loved music, had suffered through a long, debilitating illness. During the struggle, he always told his wife, "You know we sang in the sunshine. We'll sing in the rain." The music had tremendous significance and meaning for close friends and family who knew the story.

Many experts lament the substitution of memorial services for funerals. They believe this dilutes the power of the ritual, that looking at the body of the one you love is, for many people, a key component in the ability to accept and express deep grief. "Memorial services are being postponed to a more convenient time, weeks or months later, when people need a catharsis of grief now," observes a psychologist.

Guests customarily sign a memorial register, which is usually present at the funeral or memorial service, as well as at other events like calling hours. Occasionally people will add a comment, such as, "I'll never forget Sam, my mentor." In some parts of the country you may be asked to add your address, enabling the bereaved to easily send acknowledgments. If you signed the book at a visitation, you don't have to sign it again at the funeral.

Occasionally, memory cards are distributed at a funeral, allowing guests to write down a recollection of the deceased, which is later given to the family. Such shared memories are treasured. A widow sums it up this way: "If my house was on fire, I'd get my daughter out. Next would be all the memories written at the funeral about my husband."

Guidance on What to Say and Do When

When you see or talk to the bereaved for the first time after the death, express condolences. If you're in doubt about the right words, simply state, "I'm sorry." If you wish, you can add, "How can I help?" or "Tell me what I can do." In early contact, it is even sufficient to make your presence known through a touch on the arm (or a hug if your relationship makes this appropriate). What counts is that you are there; you are taking time out of your day. Your presence is more important than what you say or do.

Relatives and intimate friends may be needed from the start and will want to call or go to the home of the bereaved as soon as they hear about the death. There may be phones or doorbells to be answered, people to be notified, and arrangements to be made. When one woman lost her son and had no one else to turn to, the son's friend accompanied her to pick out the casket.

If you're not close, whether or not to call before the funeral depends on factors such as whether you have specific help to offer. A neighbor might pick up (or put up) out-of-town relatives arriving for the funeral. On the other hand, calls or visits from people who are not intimates at this time can be intrusive, especially when there are so many decisions and arrangements to be made. Follow the directions in the newspaper death notice and use your good sense and judgment. For example, grieving elderly widows or widowers, single parents, or others alone need all the support they can get. Friends and neighbors can perform an important service by organizing support.

Call, too, if you want to attend the funeral, but can't. "When my mother died," someone told me, "a relative called at the funeral home just to say that he couldn't be there. That was a nice thing to do."

After the burial, people usually return to the home of the bereaved or attend a reception of some kind elsewhere. At such a time, remember that everybody grieves differently. Some like to be among people and welcome light conversation that distracts; others retreat to a room. Take your clue from the circumstances and use good judgment. You have to know the person and know yourself. If you are not an intimate, keep your visit brief. Say, "I'm sorry," if you haven't already done so. Add, if you wish, "If there's anything I can do, I'm there for you."

Whatever you do, don't give advice, as in, "I know people who had the same thing. You really should . . ." Don't ask, "Did Johnny (who died in an auto accident) wear a seat belt?" Knowing he didn't might help reassure you that you'll be protected if you are belted, but such questions are offensive to the mourner. Do not inquire, "Was there a lot of blood?" Skip questions like "Are you going to sue?" It isn't anyone's business.

Visiting those who grieve is an important ritual and appropriate whether you're close or not. *Shiva* (the first seven days of mourning for Jews) usually starts right after the burial. Shiva is a time to pay your respects to the bereaved—and takes place in the home of a family member. Plan to stay about twenty minutes. There are no particular hours, although some families do list times in the obituary, or have them announced at the funeral. If a time is not mentioned, just use good sense, avoiding mealtimes or late-night visits.

When visiting any bereaved, just be there and give the person an opportunity to talk. You can say, "I'm here to listen anytime you want to talk" or simply, "I care about you. I'm concerned." It's the right thing to share recollections of the deceased and what the person meant to you.

Over time there's a discrepancy between the amount of support the bereaved needs and what they get. Visits and calls drop off dramatically after a few weeks. People assume, incorrectly, that the person is back to normal, or tire of rehashing the same sad memories. If you care about the individual, stay in touch. Ask how things are going.

Calls at holidays like Thanksgiving or Christmas are important, too. Because these are family times, they're painful reminders that the loved one is no longer present.

There may be some kind of ritual on the anniversary of the death, even an annual remembrance when people may, for example, light a candle. For Catholics, a Mass may be celebrated the first month after death and on the first anniversary. In the Jewish religion, an unveiling of the stone at the cemetery is commonly held eleven months after the death. You go to an unveiling, however, only if you are invited.

Flowers, Food, Contributions

A financial planner received few condolence notes when her father died. She was on leave from her job and taking care of him in a part of the world where people didn't know what happened and she didn't tell them. She felt extremely touched when she did get flowers from a group of coworkers who were aware of the situation. "I have never forgotten my positive feelings about that gesture," she says.

Flowers can be sent to the funeral home, the church, or the bereaved's home. (You can ask the family for their preference.) The accompanying card might read something like "Love from Phyllis and Guy" or "Our deepest sympathy, Jane and Bob Jones." Flowers are not generally appropriate for Jewish families, although you can sometimes send them for Reform Jewish funerals.

Another option is food, which people often send to the family's home to free the bereaved to take care of what they have to. "When my mother died, people brought food over as soon as they heard, before the memorial service as major grieving was going on," recalls one woman. When people are in shock it becomes too difficult to plan meals for the family or for oneself.

A Mass card (for a Mass to be said in memory of the person who died) is available at any parish—and can be sent if the deceased was a devout Catholic. Although a contribution is not required, it is usual to donate anywhere from ten to fifteen dollars.

A contribution in memory of the deceased is always appropriate. Frequently the obituary says something like "In lieu of flowers, donations may be sent to (a hospital, charity, or educational or arts institution)." Usually the organization had some special meaning for or connection to the deceased. One couple established a cancer research fund at a university in memory of their child. Sometimes you can contribute to a memorial scholarship. How much should you give? Figure out what you'd pay for flowers and write a check for that amount (more if you're using the contribution as a tax deduction).

People often mistakenly believe that a contribution (and the acknowledgment of your gift sent to the bereaved by the charity) replaces a condolence note. It does not. If you wish, however, you can say in your note that you've made a contribution.

Fast Facts on Religions

- *Buddhism.* A Buddhist funeral may involve a Japanese, Chinese, Vietnamese, or other Asian family, for example. Burial or cremation may follow. At some Buddhist funerals, you may see a special register (called Koden) where guests list the contribution they intend to make to help defray the family's funeral expenses. It's a form of social insurance. The amount varies, depending on your finances and your relationship with the deceased and the family, but twenty to fifty dollars is a typical range for contributions.

- *Islam.* The funeral is held within seventy-two hours of death. Muslims are always buried, never cremated. There is no set period of mourning. It is not traditional to send flowers to the funeral, but you can send a gift basket of food to the family afterward. Even better, take up a collection at the office and present the money after the burial or when you visit the home (especially if it's a husband, often the primary wage earner for the family, who has died). You can also add your donation to the contribution to the mosque which is made by family members.

- *Hindu.* You can call or visit the family before the funeral (and bring flowers then). Funerals are usually held within a day of the death. Hindus cremate. Guests can attend the cremation, which takes place after the funeral service.

Although this chapter generally covers what you need to know, each culture has its own rules and traditions. There are variations in sects within the same religion and regional differences. Only close family members usually attend the interment of a Quaker, for example. In the western part of the United States, visitation tends to be more informal (people just drop in) than in the East, where families tend to spend more time at the funeral home during specified hours.

When in doubt, call the funeral home for information. Or ask a family member.

A Guide to Eulogies

Eulogies are speeches or written tributes praising someone who has died. They have become more common in recent years, probably in reaction to the fading of so many other rituals surrounding death. Friends and relatives used to sit around informally after someone died, talking about the person. It happened spontaneously, answering a deep human need to speak well of the dead. Today, however, such personal contact often gets lost. Everyone is rushed for time; people move frequently (before they can establish deep ties); many families are scattered. There is a need for formal rhetoric.

If you're a close friend, relative, coworker, or other associate of someone who has died, you may be asked by the grieving family to give a eulogy at the funeral or memorial service. If you pale at the thought, stop a minute and realize that you don't have to be an orator to give a touching or stirring eulogy. What people want to hear is honest, human feeling. Some of the most poignant, eulogies are "unpolished"—words from the heart from people who will never win awards for public speaking. What counts, and affects the audience deeply, is their sincerity. A good eulogy has something caring and enlightening to say about the deceased. It is a gift to family and friends that leaves a lasting memory of who the person was.

Eulogy Techniques

Here's how to find words that memorialize the deceased, bring solace to family and friends, and help make sense of someone's life and loss.

A eulogy should be a salute to someone composed of words that console and admire. To make yours memorable, keep it warm and personal. There are ways to do that even if you are speaking in an official capacity (such as a police chief or a division president) and barely know or never met the person. A good eulogy talks about how that person lived his or her life, obstacles that may have been overcome, and what the person meant to family and others and to you.

It also elicits a response from family and friends. As one minister told me, "A eulogy is an affirmation of a faith tradition, together with the person's life, so the whole thing has a chance to be a cathartic experience, which is important. If grief comes out, then celebration of the person's life can take place."

Research the Person's History

Ask yourself, "Who is this person?" You must know something about the individual to write an effective eulogy. If you had a close personal or professional relationship with the person, you already have a reservoir of information to draw from. If not, or to fill in gaps, talk to the family. Ask for details (such as nicknames) that help paint a complete picture of the person, which you can then lace throughout your eulogy. Ask questions such as "Was he/she in the military (or married)?" "Did he/she have children or grandchildren?"

The answers may allow you to talk about the person's devotion to country or to family, as in "He was married for twenty-four years to his beloved wife Judy." You can reflect on the children, as in "How proud he was of his sons John and Ralph." Or, "Mack was a tough guy who had a gentle, loving side. Who can forget how he doted on his daughters." People relate to such details.

Be sure to get them from the right people, however, and corroborate the facts. In one eulogy, the speaker made several inaccurate statements about the deceased. She had talked to the wrong person, someone who didn't know the deceased all that well.

Use other sources, too. When a colleague or subordinate has died, you can search company personnel records for information on length of service, awards, or meritorious citations. Such facts captivate people and console family members.

One dedicated, experienced eulogy writer went a step further. He traced the deceased's background through government agencies, finally tracking down Vietnam records. He was then able to say, "He served his country ably in Vietnam, as well as being a heroic paramedic."

You want to conjure up the essence of the person in your eulogy, which means mentioning those broad characteristics that defined the individual, such as "He was generous. He was courageous. He was honest. He was the ultimate organizer." But it's also very effective to give examples. Try something like "When I lost my job, he was the first person to offer me a loan" or "Even when he knew he was fighting a losing battle with his illness, he never grew bitter. He chose to focus instead on his blessings in life." The listeners nod their heads in agreement and think, "Yes, that was Tim. That's the way he was."

Say why you admired or loved the person. Statements like "He was rich and he was poor, but he always came out on top" help people to feel a connection with the deceased. Broadcaster Bob Costas cemented such connection in his eulogy for Mickey Mantle, calling the baseball great ". . . a presence in our lives—a fragile hero to whom we had an emotional attachment so strong and lasting that it defied logic. Mickey often said he didn't understand it, this enduring connection and affection—the men now in their 40s and 50s, otherwise perfectly sensible, who went dry in the mouth and stammered like schoolboys in the presence of Mickey Mantle."

He went on to say ". . . Mickey Mantle had those dual qualities so seldom seen—exuding dynamism and excitement, but at the same time touching your heart—flawed, wounded. We knew there was something poignant about Mickey Mantle before we knew what poignant meant. We didn't just root for him, we felt for him." (See Appendix A for the complete eulogy.)

A discussion of the person's interests and passions also connects us as in, "She was full of surprises: a woman who loved the opera, the racetrack, and canasta, in that order." Or "We all know he was crazy about motorcycles. We called him the world's oldest Hell's Angel."

Eulogies at the funeral for a college student made him real because people spoke to who he was. He was an amateur chef who cooked meals for his fraternity brothers. He was such a devoted friend that you could call him at 3 P.M. or 3 A.M. and he'd be there for you.

One man reflected on his relationship with the deceased, someone twenty years older who was a father figure. Having lost his own father, the speaker had looked up to the older man for his wisdom and knowledge. At the funeral, he said, "I would have been proud to be his son."

In a eulogy for her eighty-seven-year-old aunt, a niece spoke of their relationship this way: "She was direct and no-nonsense and you knew just where you stood with her. Where I stood was on firm ground. She and I were good friends from way back." (See Appendix A for the complete eulogy.)

Use anecdotes, reminiscences, recollections, as in, "Going to dinner with him was always a scene. As soon as the waitress appeared to take his order, his first words were, 'Leave the lettuce off my plate. I can't stand lettuce.' He'd go anywhere, as long as they served zucchini pancakes."

In a glowing tribute to her mother-in-law who had been more of a mother to her than her own mother—and a loving grandmother to her children—a young wife said "I remember one day showing up at her house after the boys had spent the weekend with her to find chairs throughout the house and strings and clamps hooked to the chairs. She had purchased a toy called Skyracers and had placed the towers strategically throughout the house and the boys were sending her notes from across the room on their racer tramway. They had so much fun together and looked forward to their many visits with her. She had such a young heart." (See Appendix A for the complete eulogy.)

Try quotes. For someone who knew how to dream and/or achieved a great deal, you might try this one from *The Quotable Woman:*

> *Reach high, for stars lie hidden in your soul.*
> *Dream deep, for every dream precedes the goal.*
> —Pamela Vaull Starr

In an outstanding eulogy I heard at a funeral years ago, the speaker described the deceased's zest and energy with "His motto was, 'Eat dessert. Life is very uncertain.'" I've never forgotten it.

Be Honest

Look at the circumstances surrounding the death. If it was a suicide or a tragic early demise, you can't just say, "It was a good life and it was time." It wasn't time. That doesn't mean you shine a flashlight in the family's eyes and say, "Doris jumped out the window." But you can say something like "This is a tragedy. We all ask, 'Why?'" because it's true.

It's a special heartbreak when someone is taken suddenly, especially if the two of you had a rocky relationship. Yet you can give a ringing tribute, talking about what the person loved, such as a job. You might mention how the distance between you makes the death particularly difficult to accept. The honesty doesn't detract from the eulogy. It enhances its power.

One man described coming to terms with his relationship with his deeply depressed mother. He said in his eulogy, "She had . . . suffered so much from the facts of her life that she found it easier to reject uncomfortable truths and create, instead, her own, more palatable version of reality. Since she was still my mother, the woman who gave me life and nurtured me when I was little and helpless, I decided to accept her on those terms, as difficult as that often was." (See Appendix A for the complete eulogy.)

If someone died after long and difficult treatment for cancer, you might acknowledge that and include "To the end she was a heroine. Even when she was bald from chemotherapy and lesser mortals would have curled up in a ball, she was ready to join you for lunch, hooked up to her pain medication."

Honesty about the deceased's flaws can work, too, as long as compassion is part of the equation. If a suicide was a known alcoholic and a tortured soul, a eulogy might say, "Life was such a torment to him. Everyone doesn't have the ability to lead their lives and control themselves." The point is, someone has just lost a loved one. You want to honor the deceased in a way that's appropriate and shows the depth of suffering.

Use Humor Where Appropriate

At funerals it's wonderful to be able to laugh at something meaningful, including little situations where the deceased said or did something funny. It warms the occasion and breaks the tension. Some of the best eulogies create an emotional connection to the deceased with a few well-placed occasions for chuckles. You can feel tears or joy in a memory, as in "He was a happy guy, grouchy only when the Chargers lost."

If the person had a great sense of humor, evoke it. The family needs to remember special moments because the person is gone forever. What they have left are memories and their love. The person's enjoyment of life is something they can hold onto.

One eulogy began with "Who ever heard of a dentist who was funny. Jeff broke the mold. How many dinner parties did he hold in the palm of his hand as he regaled guests with his latest repertoire. And his jokes were always a riot."

Get Creative

One woman used the ABC's as a device to eulogize her grandfather. She listed twenty-six things he loved, as in "He loved *almond* ice cream, always on a sugar cone. He loved *baseball* and never missed a Mets game until his health deteriorated. He loved my grandmother *Clarisse*, the light of his life and his wife of fifty-one years." And so on.

Leave room for spontaneity, too. It's okay to depart from the written text and speak off-the-cuff. In many of the best eulogies, speakers deviate from what they've planned to say and go with an aside or anecdote that pops into mind. The unplanned quality adds power because of the obvious openness and sincerity.

If you read the entire eulogy, you'll be less effective than if you speak directly to the audience, making eye contact. If you're working off remarks, memorize as much as possible. One official makes a list of bulleted thoughts that he wants to cover and rehearses the eulogy beforehand.

Format

A eulogy should be brief, five to seven minutes is sufficient, and no more than ten. In one case, three family members locked in rivalry competed to see who could give the longest eulogy. The last was a forty-five-minute oration. The audience sat there yawning, wondering when it would finally end.

If you're not a close relative or friend, but rather something like an official of the company that employed the deceased, thank the family for allowing you to speak. Be sincere and avoid a strictly chronological approach where you list the steps in the person's career. It can get boring.

You can close your eulogy in several ways. Try "God bless him/her," if that feels right to you. "Rest in peace," "We love you, Jane," or "We'll miss you, Scott" are also fitting. Or think of what the person might be thinking or doing right now, as in "Knowing Uncle Ralph, he's probably up there right now, grinning to see all of his family and friends here together. You know how he loved a party. Good-bye, dear Uncle." A "toast" works, too, as in "Here's to you, Bob."

In his eulogy for John F. Kennedy Jr., at the Church of St. Thomas More in New York City on July 23, 1999, Senator Edward M. Kennedy skillfully used quotes (from both the deceased and his late father) and a number of anecdotes to paint a true and indelible portrait of his nephew. He closed by reciting (and commenting on) a poem that had great meaning for the occasion. Some of the most effective moments blended memory with humor: "Once, when they asked

John what he would do if he went into politics and was elected President, he said: 'I guess the first thing is call up Uncle Teddy and gloat.' I loved that. It was so like his father." (See Appendix A for the complete eulogy.)

Say Something Unique

If there is more than one eulogy, try to avoid a situation where everyone says the same thing. Every person has a different speaking style and comes from a different perspective. Capitalize on that. Some of the most stirring eulogies have been given for firefighters who have died in the line of duty. The mayor may speak, along with the fire commissioner, a union representative, and members of the firefighter's ladder company. Each has something different to bring to the eulogy.

Three New York City firefighters died on December 18, 1998 while attempting to save elderly victims who were trapped in a blazing building. Here is part of the eulogy given by Battalion Chief James McCarthy for one of the men:

> Some years ago, my daughter gave me a book in which I found the following text. It was published originally in Fortune magazine . . . I'd like to read it now.
>
> > *The manager administers, the leader innovates. The manager maintains, the leader develops. The manager relies on systems, the leader relies on people. The manager counts on controls, the leader counts on trust. The*

> *manager does things right, the leader does
> the right thing.*

Lt. Joseph Cavalieri always did the right thing.
He was a great leader. . . .

The eulogy went on to speak of Lt. Cavalieri's
rescue of a child from a burning building, his relationship with coworkers, family, and community. (See
Appendix A for more of the eulogy.)

In the case of a firefighter, you can talk about ultimate sacrifice and draw on several hundred years of
tradition. However, when I gave a eulogy for my own
father, I was talking about someone who was *not* a
hero, just a man. I used that as a way of offering insight
into his soul. I also explained why I loved him. I said,
in part:

"My father was a simple man with a good heart,
who led an ordinary life. Yet he was a man who had
dreams and he taught me to have them. When I was
growing up in Brooklyn, I remember that he always
dreamed of winning the Irish Sweepstakes. Every year
he'd buy a ticket and say, 'This is the year. I'm going to
win this time.' And I always believed him. I spent so
many hours of my childhood staring out of my bedroom window, fantasizing about what we'd do with all
that money when his ticket came through. He never
did win. But that didn't matter. What mattered was
that he gave me the gift of possibility." (See Appendix
A for the complete eulogy.)

Try not to gloss over the more challenging traits
of the deceased's personality. It is possible to remember someone who might have been most well
known for complaining. This is part of a eulogy I

wrote for an eighty-four-year-old artist friend: "Karl was an original. In this age of the "bland" and "politically" "correct," he was an unvarnished curmudgeon. 'This is who I am,' he (and his art) seemed to say, 'Like it or not.'" (See Appendix A for the complete eulogy.)

You don't need a special talent to say good-bye in a meaningful way. You just have to do your homework and let your heart speak freely. When you do, you bring comfort to the family and to yourself.

Appendix A

Eulogy for Mickey Mantle
by Bob Costas

You know, it occurs to me as we're all sitting here
thinking of Mickey, he's probably somewhere getting
an earful from Casey Stengel, and no doubt quite con-
fused by now.

One of Mickey's fondest wishes was that he be
remembered as a great teammate, to know that the men
he played with thought well of him. But it was more
than that. Moose and Whitey and Tony and Yogi and
Bobby and Hank, what a remarkable team you were.
And the stories of the visits you guys made to Mickey's
bedside the last few days were heartbreakingly tender.
It meant everything to Mickey, as would the presence
of so many baseball figures past and present here
today.

I was honored to be asked to speak by the Mantle
family today. I am not standing here as a broadcaster.

Mel Allen is the eternal voice of the Yankees and that would be his place. And there are others here with a longer and deeper association with Mickey than mine.

But I guess I'm here, not so much to speak for myself as to simply represent the millions of baseball-loving kids who grew up in the '50s and '60s and for whom Mickey Mantle was baseball.

And more than that, he was a presence in our lives—a fragile hero to whom we had an emotional attachment so strong and lasting that it defied logic. Mickey often said he didn't understand it, this enduring connection and affection—the men now in their forties and fifties, otherwise perfectly sensible, who went dry in the mouth and stammered like schoolboys in the presence of Mickey Mantle.

Maybe Mick was uncomfortable with it, not just because of his basic shyness, but because he was always too honest to regard himself as some kind of deity. But that was never really the point. In a very different time than today, the first baseball commissioner, Kenesaw Mountain Landis, said, "Every boy builds a shrine to some baseball hero, and before that shrine, a candle always burns."

For a huge portion of my generation, Mickey Mantle was that baseball hero. And for reasons that no statistics, no dry recitation of the facts can possibly capture, he was the most compelling baseball hero of our lifetime. And he was our symbol of baseball at a time when the game meant something to us that perhaps it no longer does.

Mickey Mantle had those dual qualities so seldom seen—exuding dynamism and excitement, but at the same time touching your heart—flawed, wounded. We knew there was something poignant about Mickey Mantle before we knew what *poignant* meant. We didn't just root for him, we felt for him.

Long before many of us ever cracked a serious book, we knew something about mythology as we watched Mickey Mantle run out a home run through the lengthening shadows of a late Sunday afternoon at Yankee Stadium.

There was a greatness in him, but a vulnerability too. He was our guy. When he was hot, we felt great. When he slumped or got hurt, we sagged a bit too. We tried to crease our caps like him; kneel in an imaginary on-deck circle like him; run like him, heads down, elbows up.

Billy Crystal is here today. Billy says that at his bar mitzvah he spoke in an Oklahoma drawl. Billy's here today because he loved Mickey Mantle, and millions more who felt like him are here today in spirit as well.

It's been said that the truth is never pure and rarely simple. Mickey Mantle was too humble and honest to believe that the whole truth about him could be found on a Wheaties box or a baseball card. But the emotional truths of childhood have a power that transcends objective fact. They stay with us through all the years, withstanding the ambivalence that so often accompanies the experience of adults.

That's why we can still recall the immediate tingle in that instant of recognition when a Mickey Mantle popped up in a pack of Topps bubble gum cards—a treasure lodged between an Eli Grba and a Pumpsie Green.

That's why we smile today, recalling those October afternoons when we'd sneak a transistor radio into school to follow Mickey and the Yankees in the World Series.

Or when I think of Mr. Tomasi, a very wise sixth-grade teacher who understood that the World Series was more important, at least for one day, than any school lesson could be. So he brought his black and white TV from home, plugged it in and let us watch it right there in school through the flicker and the static. It was richer and more compelling than anything I've seen on a high-resolution, big-screen TV.

Of course, the bad part, Bobby, was that Koufax struck 15 of you guys out that day.

My phone's been ringing the past few weeks as Mickey fought for his life. I've heard from people I hadn't seen or talked to in years—guys I played stick-ball with, even some guys who took Willie's side in those endless Mantle–Mays arguments. They're grown up now. They have their families. They're not even necessarily big baseball fans anymore. But they felt something hearing about Mickey, and they figured I did too.

In the last year, Mickey Mantle, always so hard on himself, finally came to accept and appreciate that distinction between a role model and a hero. The first he often was not, the second he always will be.

And, in the end, people got it. And Mickey Mantle got from America something other than misplaced and mindless celebrity worship. He got something far more meaningful. He got love—love for what he had been, love for what he made us feel, love for the humanity and sweetness that was always there mixed in with the flaws and all the pain that racked his body and his soul.

We wanted to tell him that it was OK, that what he had been was enough. We hoped he felt that Mutt

Mantle would have understood and that Merlyn and the boys loved him. And then in the end, something remarkable happened—the way it does for champions. Mickey Mantle rallied. His heart took over, and he had some innings as fine as any in 1956 or with his buddy, Roger, in 1961.

But this time, he did it in the harsh and trying summer of '95. And what he did was stunning. The sheer grace of that ninth inning—the humility, the sense of humor, the total absence of self pity, the simple eloquence and honesty of his pleas to others to take heed of his mistakes.

All of America watched in admiration. His doctors said he was, in many ways, the most remarkable patient they'd ever seen. His bravery so stark and real, that even those used to seeing people in dire circumstances were moved by his example.

Because of that example, organ donations are up dramatically all across America. A cautionary tale has been honestly told and perhaps will affect some lives for the better.

And our last memories of Mickey Mantle are as heroic as the first. None of us, Mickey included, would want to be held to account for every moment of our lives. But how many of us could say that our best moments were as magnificent as his?

This is a cartoon from this morning's *Dallas Morning News*. Maybe some of you saw it. It got torn a little bit on the way from the hotel to here. There's a figure here, St. Peter I take it to be, with his arm around Mickey, that broad back and the number 7. He's holding his book of admissions. He says, "Kid, that was the most courageous ninth inning I've ever seen."

It brings to mind a story Mickey liked to tell on

himself and maybe some of you have heard it. He pictured himself at the pearly gates, met by St. Peter, who shook his head and said, "Mick, we checked the record. We know some of what went on. Sorry, we can't let you in, but before you go, God wants to know if you'd sign these six dozen baseballs."

Well, there were days when Mickey Mantle was so darn good that we kids would bet that even God would want his autograph. But like the cartoon says, I don't think Mick needed to worry much about the other part.

I just hope God has a place for him where he can run again. Where he can play practical jokes on his teammates and smile that boyish smile, 'cause God knows, no one's perfect. And God knows there's something special about heroes.

So long, Mick. Thanks.

Eulogy for John F. Kennedy Jr.
by Senator Edward M. Kennedy

Thank you, President and Mrs. Clinton and Chelsea, for being here today. You've shown extraordinary kindness throughout the course of this week.

Once, when they asked John what he would do if he went into politics and was elected President, he said: "I guess the first thing is call up Uncle Teddy and gloat." I loved that. It was so like his father.

From the first day of his life, John seemed to belong not only to our family, but to the American family.

The whole world knew his name before he did.

A famous photograph showed John racing across the lawn as his father landed in the White House helicopter and swept up John in his arms. When my brother saw that photo, he exclaimed, "Every mother in the United States is saying, 'Isn't it wonderful to see that love between a son and his father, the way that John races to be with his father.' Little do they know—that son would have raced right by his father to get to that helicopter."

But John was so much more than those long-ago images emblazoned in our minds. He was a boy who grew into a man with a zest for life and a love of adventure. He was a pied piper who brought us all along. He was blessed with a father and mother who never thought anything mattered more than their children.

When they left the White House, Jackie's soft and gentle voice and unbreakable strength of spirit guided him surely and securely to the future. He had a legacy, and he learned to treasure it. He was part of a legend, and he learned to live with it. Above all, Jackie gave him a place to be himself, to grow up, to laugh and cry, to dream and strive on his own.

John learned that lesson well. He had amazing grace. He accepted who he was, but he cared more about what he could and should become. He saw things that could be lost in the glare of the spotlight. And he could laugh at the absurdity of too much pomp and circumstance.

He loved to travel across this city by subway, bicycle, and roller blade. He lived as if he were unrecognizable—although he was known by everyone he encountered. He always introduced himself, rather than take anything for granted. He drove his own car and flew his own plane, which is how he wanted it. He was the king of his domain. He thought politics should be an integral part of our popular culture, and that popular culture should be an integral part of politics. He transformed that belief into the creation of *George*. John shaped and honed a fresh, often irreverent, journal. His new political magazine attracted a new generation, many of whom had never read about politics before.

John also brought to *George* a wit that was quick and sure. The premier issue of *George* caused a stir with a cover photograph of Cindy Crawford dressed as George Washington with a bare belly button. The "Reliable Source" in the *Washington Post* printed a mock cover of *George* showing not Cindy Crawford, but me dressed as George Washington, with my belly button exposed. I suggested to John that perhaps I should have been the model for the first cover of his magazine. Without missing a beat, John told me that he stood by his original editorial decision.

John brought this same playful wit to other aspects of his life. He campaigned for me during my 1994 election and always caused a stir when he arrived in Massachusetts. Before one of his trips to Boston, John told the campaign he was bringing along a companion, but would need only one hotel room.

Interested, but discreet, a senior campaign worker picked John up at the airport and prepared to handle any media barrage that might accompany John's arrival with his mystery companion. John landed with the companion alright—an enormous German shepherd dog named Sam he had just rescued from the pound.

He loved to talk about the expression on the campaign worker's face and the reaction of the clerk at the Charles Hotel when John and Sam checked in.

I think now not only of these wonderful adventures, but of the kind of person John was. He was the son who quietly gave extraordinary time and ideas to the Institute of Politics at Harvard that bears his father's name. He brought to the Institute his distinctive insight that politics could have a broader appeal, that it was not just about elections, but about the larger forces that shape our whole society.

John was also the son who was once protected by his mother. He went on to become her pride—and then her protector in her final days. He was the Kennedy who loved us all, but who especially cherished his sister Caroline, celebrated her brilliance, and took strength and joy from their lifelong mutual admiration society.

And for a thousand days, he was a husband who adored the wife who became his perfect soul-mate. John's father taught us all to reach for the moon and the stars. John did that in all he did—and he found his shining star when he married Carolyn Bessette.

How often our family will think of the two of them, cuddling affectionately on a boat—surrounded by family—aunts—uncles—Caroline and Ed and their children, Rose, Tatiana, and Jack—Kennedy cousins—Radizwill cousins—Shriver cousins—Smith cousins—Lawford cousins—as we sailed Nantucket Sound.

Then we would come home — and before dinner, on the lawn where his father had played, John would lead a spirited game of touch football—and his beautiful young wife, the new pride of the Kennedys, would cheer for John's team and delight her nieces and nephews with her somersaults.

We loved Carolyn. She and her sister Lauren were young extraordinary women of high accomplishment

—and their own limitless possibilities. We mourn their loss and honor their lives. The Bessette and Freeman families will always be part of ours.

John was a serious man who brightened our lives with his smile and his grace. He was a son of privilege who founded a program called "Reaching Up," to train better care-givers for the mentally disabled. He joined Wall Street executives on the Robin Hood Foundation to help the city's impoverished children. And he did it all so quietly, without ever calling attention to himself.

John was one of Jackie's two miracles. He was still becoming the person he would be, and doing it by the beat of his own drummer. He had only just begun. There was in him a great promise of things to come.

The Irish ambassador recited a poem to John's father and mother soon after John was born. I can hear it again now, at this different and difficult moment:

We wish to the new child
A heart that can be beguiled
By a flower
That the wind lifts
As it passes.
If the storms break for him,
May the trees shake for him
Their blossoms down.

In the night that he is troubled,
May a friend wake for him,
So that his time be doubled,
And at the end of all loving and love,
May the Man above
Give him a crown.

We thank the millions who have rained blossoms down on John's memory.

He and his bride have gone to be with his mother and father, where there will never be an end to love. He was lost on that troubled night—but we will always wake for him, so that his time, which was not doubled, but cut in half, will live forever in our memory, and in our beguiled and broken hearts.

We dared to think, in that other Irish phrase, that this John Kennedy would live to comb grey hair, with his beloved Carolyn by his side. But like his father, he had every gift but length of years.

We who have loved him from the day he was born, and watched the remarkable man he became, now bid him farewell. God bless you, John and Carolyn. We love you, and we always will.

Eulogy for Lt. Joseph Cavalieri by Battalion Chief James McCarthy

Some years ago, my daughter gave me a book in which I found the following text. It was published originally in *Fortune* magazine . . . I'd like to read it now. "The manager administers, the leader innovates. The manager maintains, the leader develops. The manager relies on systems, the leader relies on people. The manager counts on controls, the leader counts on trust. The manager does things right, the leader does the right thing."

Lt. Joseph Cavalieri *always* did the right thing. He was a great leader.

I first met Joe when I arrived in L-150, back in 1990. On one of my first tours . . . Joe asked me if I would mind if he told me a little about the house. He told me how the companies prided themselves in taking care of their rigs and the firehouse, and how both companies got along so well together. He gave me a lowdown on the types of operations often encountered; the buildings in the area; the high false alarm rate and many other things. . . . I came to respect his opinion on almost every subject we discussed.

Joe was gifted with a sensational sense of humor. Countless stories were told over the last few days. Joe was mischievous, whether it was hiding his lieutenant's meal, or preparing to dowse someone, or cream-pieing the face of a birthday boy, or tickling people. He was always stirring the pot, always laughing.

He was recognized by the Board of Merit for two rescues he made while at L-150. I personally wrote up his rescue of a small girl who was left in a burning building while the other members of her family were able to escape. I saw this big man tenderly cradle the limp body and carry her to the ambulance. And he stayed with the girl until he was sure she would recover.

He was good at a fire. But he was also good in the office, good in the kitchen. He also became an excellent training officer.

Joe was a clean-living, religious person. His personal conduct could serve as an example to all of us. As the Holy Name delegate he always got many of the members to attend communion breakfasts. He was also a valued community leader. I was given a long list of his civic accomplishments. Some of them: headed the youth board and took the kids on many trips; was involved with soccer and basketball. He was responsible for the events board in the center of town.

Joe was a member of a very close family. He was devoted to his mother and mother-in-law . . . He has three brothers, and many nieces and nephews. A brother-in-law, Chris, is also a firefighter.

If you knew Joe, you knew of his love and devotion and pride in his lovely daughters. They were the light of his life . . . Meagan, attending Fordham University, and Maureen, getting ready for high school.

Twenty-four years ago, Joe married his childhood sweetheart. No words that I can say can describe their love. It was boundless.

I spoke about his leadership—humor—courage—dedication—determination—his religious convictions—his community life—and his family life. All little parts of that *great big man*.

Lt. Joseph Cavalieri of the New York City Fire Department—a beautiful man—a hero—a good fireman—and my friend.

Eulogy for My Father

My father was a simple man with a good heart, who led an ordinary life. Yet he was a man who had dreams—and he taught me to have them. When I was growing up in Brooklyn, I remember that he always dreamed of winning the Irish Sweepstakes. Every year he'd buy a ticket and say, "This is the year. I'm going to win this time." And I always believed him. I spent so many hours of my childhood staring out of my bedroom window, fantasizing about what we'd do with all that money when his ticket came through.

He never did win. But that didn't matter. What mattered was that he gave me the gift of possibility. He had dreams for all his children and he always told us, "You can be anything you want to be, do anything you want to do, if you're willing to work for it." Many of his own dreams were never fulfilled, but we fulfilled many of ours.

Several years ago, before his life had been narrowed so much by his failing health, he told me he had always wanted to go to Australia. A long, hard trip like that became impossible. He never saw Australia. That was another dream unrealized. It's not surprising that I want to go to Australia some day, too.

My father was a simple man who led an ordinary life, yet this ordinary man never lost the child in himself. He knew how to play. He made up the best stories and told them to me and to my children. Some of his finest hours as a father took place during those long summers of my childhood, when we ran away from the heat and the terror of polio in those days to a bungalow colony in the Catskills.

Families stayed the whole summer. But fathers had to work at their jobs all week in the city. The kids lined up along the side of the road on Friday nights, waiting for the parade of headlights in the dark—our fathers in their cars driving back for the weekend. They all brought presents, but my father chose the best ones—precious little items from the five and dime: paddle-balls, spaldeens for punch ball, jump ropes, jacks and Crayola crayons. He brought us the best comic books, knowing intuitively which ones were the best—the ones every kid wanted.

I know somehow that you're up there, right now Dad, watching us and smiling. I hope you're playing gin—and winning.

Eulogy for Karl Fortess

There's an ache in my heart as I speak to you today. Karl was an original. In this age of the "bland" and "politically correct," he was an unvarnished curmudgeon. "This is who I am," he (and his art) seemed to say, "Like it or not."

Some people didn't like Karl. He was not an easy man—stubborn and opinionated. Yet those were the very qualities that endeared him to others, who valued his integrity and knowledge—and the twinkle in his eye, always there if you looked.

Karl was never quite the same after his wife Lillian died. Though they often locked into tests of will, she provided an energy that helped light his way. This tension was productive; without it, he languished and the loneliness never left.

Karl regretted that he and Lillian never had children. "We meant to," he said, explaining that the timing always seemed to be wrong. He didn't have much patience and who knows what kind of a father he would have been. What he *did* possess was generosity that extended to the students he taught.

He gave to his friends, too, and to my husband and me, he brought a special spirit. He was always full of wonderful stories about the old days in Chicago and Paris—stories we wanted to hear. He was always ready to take a ride, see a movie, go to lunch—and meet a new friend, especially a female. He loved and appreciated women and, at eighty-four, captivated many of us in return.

Karl never found the kind of recognition he felt his art deserved; he lost Lillian. But in the end, he had his beloved cat "Puss," his dear friend Woody, and those of us who treasured this irascible, special friend who brought such fresh air into our lives. We love you Karl. Oh, how we'll miss you.

Eulogy for My Mother, by Marvin J. Wolf

My mother was born in Chicago in the war year of 1918, the seventh and youngest child . . . Mom married my Dad in January 1937, when she was nineteen and he a year older . . . My sister Freyda was born in 1938. I came along three years later, followed at intervals by Ted, Ila, Matt, and Steve.

One of my first memories is of sitting at a dining room table with my older sister and Mom, going through Freyda's first-grade lessons. As Freyda was taught the alphabet, I learned it, too. When she acquired addition and subtraction, Mom taught me those skills as well. Long before Montessori became a household word, my mother made sure I got a head start on the "three R's."

As more and more children arrived, however, she could no longer find time to give them what she gave me. And some time around my seventh or eighth year, I became aware that something was wrong with her. The kind, gentle, patient woman I knew became frightened and, too often, angry. As the oldest boy, I was forced to assume many more responsibilities than were usual for a child of my age, something that in hindsight I realize burdened me with adulthood while I was yet a child. It would be years before we discovered that my mother suffered from a severe form of depression and more years before science began to treat this disease with effective drugs. It was longer still before people dared to speak openly and without shame about mental illness.

My mother had a long but often unhappy life. Because of her affliction, she was forced to spend long periods away from her family in hospitals where doctors were only beginning to look for ways to treat her disease pharmaceutically. There were brief periods when she was lucid, when she could cope with her many responsibilities, and at those times the wonderful, confident, caring woman that I had loved as a little boy reappeared. More often, however, she was a mysterious stranger who reacted less and less predictably to life's little problems.

At seventeen I joined the Army. Most of my siblings also left home as soon as they could. Years later, after I was myself a father, I began to re-acquaint myself with my mother. By this time, drugs had been developed that permitted her to live, for extended periods, an almost normal life.

She had endured practically everything invented during an almost medieval era when psychotherapists used electroshock to treat their unwitting patients. She had by then suffered so much from the facts of her life that she found it easier to reject uncomfortable truths and create, instead, her own, more palatable version of reality. Since she was still my mother, the woman who gave me life and nurtured me when I was little and helpless, I decided to accept her on those terms, as difficult as that often was.

Mom liked music, as long as it wasn't too loud or too new, and so she looked forward to any excuse to visit tall buildings. She loved flowers and enjoyed watching my father cultivate the family rosebushes.

She had an almost innate sense of style. Combined with her penchant for bargain-hunting, my mother never let the lack of money stand in the way of making a fashion statement on every conceivable occasion. She greatly valued promptness; if dinner was supposed to begin at five, not even an act of Congress could have delayed her asking my father to serve the first course.

Though she never explored employment outside the home, my mother became acutely aware of just how difficult it was for waitresses and retail sales clerks to meet all the demands of their professions.

Mom had few personal ambitions in the world of business, but was devoted to giving detailed career advice and encouragement to younger people. For much of her life, she voiced strong views about national political figures and their policies. They rarely met her expectations. She was a keen observer of the efforts of people of other races and creeds to take their rightful place in American society. In her later years, she was passionately concerned with welfare issues and expended a great deal of energy grappling with the problems of the poor and disabled.

Toward the end of her life, various illnesses began to overtake her. As she became totally dependent on others, her anxieties at times overwhelmed her. As she grappled with her pain and fear, her obvious distress was heart-rending.

Now my mother is gone, and while I will miss her, I'm also relieved that her suffering is over. I'm eternally grateful for all she taught me. I treasure most the few fragments of memory that remain from my earliest years, when she was the only person in the world whom I knew would always be there for me.

Eulogy for an Aunt
by Carol Weston

When I told my four-year-old daughter that my Aunt Lisa had died, she said, "Girls don't die and neither do mothers."

I said that usually you have to be very very old to die. But what is very very old? At eighty-seven, Aunt Lisa certainly was not very very old. She was youthful and energetic. She had spunk and style. She was direct and no-nonsense, and you knew just where you stood with her.

Where I stood was on firm ground. She and I were good friends from way back. I remember when she babysat for my brothers and me when my parents were on a trip. I was 11 and we had chickens then and she helped me chase a runaway rooster around the neighborhood and back into its coop. The rooster was furious, but Aunt Lisa was unruffled.

For her, being with family was always fun, always an adventure. When I got married, she visited me in Columbus, then Chicago, then New York. My husband and I took her to the top of the World Trade Center. We never thought to slow down for her because she could always keep up. In Cape Cod we took her on a whale watch. We weren't afraid that she might get seasick or tired because she was so tough, such a trooper. When she shared a room last year with my little daughters, we didn't worry that such accommodations could be unsettling. If her great nieces woke up at dawn, she reasoned, she'd have more time to spend with them.

Aunt Lisa was such a good sport; such an ideal guest. You didn't have to censor yourself or search for things to talk about the way you do with some people who shared her age but not her spirit. Anything was a good topic of conversation—it was hard to shock Aunt Lisa. She was always interesting, and interested, and up on current events. She commanded respect. She was easy going. She had no complaints. She didn't want to be any trouble, but she did want to see and do as much as possible. And she did. Here and in England, Israel, Alaska, Hawaii.

Aunt Lisa and I wrote each other, too. Not letters. Mostly just notes. She sent me dollar-off diaper coupons; I sent her photos of the kids. Month after month.

The last time I saw her we both arrived at a party of my mother's wearing navy blue with white polka dots. Someone took a photo of us—two grown women with matching dresses and wide smiles. You look at it and you can tell we were big fans of each other.

I'm glad that Aunt Lisa lived so long and so well. I'm glad for her work, her travels, her many friends, and for the pride and love she felt for and from her family.

Edna St. Vincent Millay wrote,

Down, down, down into the darkness of the grave.
Gently they go, the beautiful, the tender, the kind;
Quietly they go, the intelligent, the witty, the brave.
I know. But I do not approve. And I am not resigned.

Do I wish Aunt Lisa had made it to 101 as did her mother, my grandmother? Of course. Yet not if it would have meant living with less dignity, less vitality, less joy.

Sometimes Aunt Lisa said with a resigned shrug, "Listen, kiddo, no one lives forever."

She got to eighty-seven. She died with her children beside her. And until she died, she lived. That is a blessing. But we will still miss her, you and I.

Eulogy for a Mother-in-Law
by Debra Dorph

Claire embraced life with all her heart and soul. She was much more than my mother-in-law, she was my best friend. Not many women can say that about their mother-in-law, but she accepted me into her life and into her family as one of her own. I used to talk to her just about every day. She was always there to listen, give me guidance when I needed it, advice if I asked for it, and her loving arms when I was struggling. She never wanted to interfere in my relationship with Abe. She would always say, "You married him. He's yours now. Or, 'I told you so.'"

This morning I spoke with my boys Jonathan and Matthew about what they remember most about their grandma. They both came up with basically the same things. They used to call her "the pancake Grandma" because whenever they stayed with her she would let them help make pancakes. They said every single time they made pancakes Grandma would not only drop the eggs, she would spill the milk. That used to crack them up and they used to anticipate it every pancake morning.

They also remember the many trips to Toys 'R' Us and Zainy Brainy she made with them on just about every visit to Grandma's. She loved Legos and making puzzles. I think sometimes she made excuses for the boys needing Legos because in reality she really wanted them herself. She would sit on the floor for hours assembling the many sets she had purchased for them.

I have had such good fortune in having such a wonderful person like Claire in my life. She taught me so many things about love, tradition, values, and morals, but most of all she taught me about how to be a good person, how to be kind, and how to love everyone. She said life was just too short for any animosity.

I remember one day showing up at her house after the boys had spent the weekend with her to find chairs throughout the house and strings and clamps hooked to the chairs. She had purchased a toy called Skyracers and had placed the towers strategically throughout the house and the boys were sending her notes from across the room on their racer tramway. They had so much fun together and looked forward to their many visits with her. She never wanted to ever grow old. She had such a young heart. She wanted to have fun and still be a kid. I know that is why her grandchildren loved her so dearly and respected her so much. She always encouraged them to be themselves and to appreciate everything there is in life and to embrace it.

She loved history and obviously instilled that love in my oldest son Jonathan when he got an A-plus on his report card this marking period.

Whenever I needed her she was always there without hesitation and with open arms to help or just to listen with a sympathetic ear. She touched so many of our lives in so many beautiful ways. She was a very special person to all of us. In conclusion I am going to recite something that Abe said to me recently about his mother. It goes like this. "My mom is the most wonderful woman I've ever known. She's never had a bit of malice in her body. Everything she's ever done she's done for love." I told Claire what Abe had said about her and she replied, "That was one of the greatest honors I've ever been given. I now feel as if I've done everything I've come to this earth to accomplish. My life is now very complete."

Claire, thanks for being such a huge part in my life. I will always remember you and I will miss you so very much. I love you.

Reference Library

Bartlett, John. *Bartlett's Familiar Quotations.* 16th ed. Justin Kaplan, ed. Boston: Little, Brown, 1992.

The Book of Eulogies. Phyllis Theroux, ed. New York: Scribner, 1997.

Dresser, Norine. *Multicultural Celebrations: Today's Rules of Etiquette for Life's Special Occasions.* New York: Three Rivers Press, 1999.

Magida, Arthur J. *How to Be a Perfect Stranger: A Guide to Etiquette in Other People's Religious Ceremonies.* Woodstock, Vt.: Jewish Lights Publishing, 1996.

Post, Peggy. *Emily Post's Etiquette.* 16th ed. New York: HarperCollins, 1997.

The Quotable Woman. Philadelphia: Running Press, 1991.

Tripp, Rhoda Thomas, comp. *The International Thesaurus of Quotations.* New York: Harper & Row, 1970.

Index